Overcoming Common Problems Series

Coping with a Mid-Life Crisis
Derek Milne

Coping with Polycystic Ovary Syndrome
Christiine Craggs-Hinton

Coping with Postnatal Depression
Sandra L. Wheatley

Coping with SAD
Fiona Marshall and Peter Cheevers

Coping with Snoring and Sleep Apnoea
Jill Eckersley

Coping with a Stressed Nervous System
Dr Kenneth Hambly and Alice Muir

Coping with Strokes
Dr Tom Smith

Coping with Suicide
Maggie Helen

Coping with Thyroid Problems
Dr Joan Gomez

Depression
Dr Paul Hauck

Depression at Work
Vicky Maud

Depressive Illness
Dr Tim Cantopher

Eating for a Healthy Heart
Robert Povey, Jacqui Morrell and Rachel Povey

Effortless Exercise
Dr Caroline Shreeve

Fertility
Julie Reid

Free Your Life from Fear
Jenny Hare

Getting a Good Night's Sleep
Fiona Johnston

Heal the Hurt: How to Forgive and Move On
Dr Ann Macaskill

Heart Attacks – Prevent and Survive
Dr Tom Smith

Help Your Child Get Fit Not Fat
Jan Hurst and Sue Hubberstey

Helping Children Cope with Anxiety
Jill Eckersley

Helping Children Cope with Change and Loss
Rosemary Wells

Helping Children Get the Most from School
Sarah Lawson

How to Be Your Own Best Friend
Dr Paul Hauck

How to Beat Pain
Christine Craggs-Hinton

How to Cope with Bulimia
Dr Joan Gomez

How to Cope with Difficult People
Alan Houel and Christian Godefroy

How to Improve Your Confidence
Dr Kenneth Hambly

How to Keep Your Cholesterol in Check
Dr Robert Povey

How to Stick to a Diet
Deborah Steinberg and Dr Windy Dryden

How to Stop Worrying
Dr Frank Tallis

Hysterectomy
Suzie Hayman

Is HRT Right for You?
Dr Anne MacGregor

Letting Go of Anxiety and Depression
Dr Windy Dryden

Lifting Depression the Balanced Way
Dr Lindsay Corrie

Living with Alzheimer's Disease
Dr Tom Smith

Living with Asperger Syndrome
Dr Joan Gomez

Living with Asthma
Dr Robert Youngson

Living with Autism
Fiona Marshall

Living with Crohn's Disease
Dr Joan Gomez

Living with Diabetes
Dr Joan Gomez

Living with Fibromyalgia
Christine Craggs-Hinton

Living with Food Intolerance
Alex Gazzola

Living with Grief
Dr Tony Lake

Overcoming Common Problems Series

Overcoming Common Problems

How to Talk to Your Child

Solving problems at home and school

PENNY OATES

sheldon PRESS

First published in Great Britain in 2007

Sheldon Press
36 Causton Street
London SW1P 4ST

British Library Cataloguing-in-Publication Data
A catalogue record for this book is available from the British Library

ISBN-13: 978–0–85969–992–1

1 3 5 7 9 10 8 6 4 2

Typeset by Northern Phototypesetting Co Ltd, Bolton
Printed in Great Britain by Ashford Colour Press, Hampshire

Contents

For my two sons, who taught me so much about parenting

Introduction

Virginia Woolf described her formative years as 'the great cathedral space which was childhood'. As a parent you want to create a stimulating, comfortable and secure space for your children. However, this is also the context in which children need to learn important and sometimes very difficult lessons about life from you if they are to grow up to become responsible adults.

Such opportunities will inevitably arise as your children navigate their way through the many milestones facing them as they strive to become increasingly independent. These may stem from something which is happening at home or at school, or perhaps in both environments, and they are part and parcel of growing up and learning to take one's place in society.

Whatever the issue, I have found that the best way to achieve a positive outcome for children is through communication. Time spent in listening and talking is never wasted. It will help you to achieve a better understanding of how, and why, any problem has arisen. It will also enable you to devise a realistic action plan which can be worked through together by those most closely involved in the situation.

In compiling this guidance I have drawn on the numerous conversations which I have had with parents over many years about how best to address the problems which they and their children are facing, and when we later reviewed the subsequent outcomes. I hope that parents will find material here which will help them to address any existing problems and also to pre-empt possible future difficulties.

It has not been possible to anticipate the substance of every conversation, so I have outlined some typical scenarios and included suggestions as to how parents might initiate a discussion.

You know your child best and will be able to determine what the priorities need to be at any given time. Remember that you run the risk of confusing your child if too many issues are tackled simultaneously, and that this can result in a no-win situation for a child. Recognize that external factors, which are beyond your own or your child's immediate control, will need to be taken into account, and give praise for any positive progress, no matter how small it may seem.

Your children's 'cathedral space' will change dramatically as they get older. By continuing to talk with them you will be able to keep abreast of some of what they are experiencing within that space and be better able to offer appropriate support when the going gets tough.

1

House rules and behavioural issues

Problems arise when your child fails to live up to expectations, but, before you chastise him, you need to be absolutely certain that he knows *how* you want him to behave and that he understands *why* the rules are important.

If you involve him in the process of agreeing boundaries and establishing the house rules, he is more likely to try to comply with them, though it is worth remembering that total compliance is unlikely. As your child gets older, the rules will need to be adapted to take into account his emotional and physical development.

Bedtime

The perfect bedtime routine is when your child goes willingly, on time and settles to sleep promptly. The reality can be somewhat different. You may be frustrated because you cannot remember when you last had a free evening. Or the teacher has said that your child appears to be tired at school, or someone has mentioned that their child goes to bed much earlier than yours.

You are not being unreasonable in insisting that your child is in bed by a certain time. No matter how loudly he tells you that he has to go to bed before all his friends, your child needs a good night's sleep and you are entitled to time to yourself. If you do not have a non-negotiable and established routine, you will have night after night of protracted debate, which will merely perpetuate the problem.

First, decide on an appropriate time for him to be in bed, but not necessarily asleep. There could be one time for school days and another for the weekend, although Sunday should be earlier, in readiness for school the next day. During the holidays, bedtimes should not count as one long weekend because children need sleep to develop healthy bodies and lively minds, and you need a break.

Once the times are agreed, the adults must adhere to them. You will need to have a conversation with your child about the change in the routine.

Say, firmly and authoritatively: *We have decided that, from now on, your bedtime will be eight o'clock on school days. This will give you plenty of time to do the things you like doing and it will also mean that you get a good night's sleep, which everyone needs to keep them healthy. Eight o'clock is the time you are to be in bed. You can read after that, but the light must be out from eight thirty.*

In all probability he will let you know, and in no uncertain terms, that he thinks this is totally unreasonable. You must stick to your decision.

Other points you might need to make are:

- You need to go to sleep at eight o'clock because you are too tired to get up in the morning.
- Mrs Bloggs has told me that you are tired at school.
- I need some time to myself in the evenings.
- You can have an extension to eight thirty on Fridays and Saturdays, because it is the weekend, but on Sunday bedtime is eight o'clock

Each time he is in bed by the appointed time, reward him by saying how pleased you are. Also tell him how much more alert he is during the following day. Always make sure that the light is out by the deadline.

If something unexpected interferes with the usual routine, explain that he will be reverting to the normal time as soon as possible. If he is consistently failing to meet the deadline, this must be addressed: *We will have to start getting you ready for bed earlier because you are not yet managing to be in bed by eight o'clock.* This should have the effect of speeding him on his way, because he will not want to start going to bed even earlier.

Some families find that their child will not sleep in his own bed. This situation will have arisen either because he has made his way into your bed, or you have brought him in during the night. You may even have allowed him to settle down for the night in your bed.

An agreed strategy will take some determination and may be quite lengthy. Begin by talking about the situation with your child: *Why do you like coming into our bed?* You may get one of the following, or even a combination of answers:

- I like being near you.
- I am afraid of the dark.
- It's warmer/more comfortable in your bed.

Listen to the answer and take each point seriously: *Thank you for telling me why you like it. I like being near you too, but night-time is when we must have a good sleep and it is better for all of us if we do this in our own beds. You are getting too big to sleep with me any more. I am going to help you feel more comfortable in your own bed. We can put a pillow in your bed so that it feels as if there is someone there with you and I will put a hot-water bottle in before you get into bed so that it feels nice and warm for you.*

Be firm and do not let him start off the night in your bed. When he arrives in your room during the night take him straight back to his own bed. However many times you need to do this, you must do it. Each time, make him comfortable, say goodnight and leave. Do not stay in the room with him, because if you do he will try to incorporate this into his routine for going to sleep. The next morning, be positive if you have grounds to be so. If not, don't mention the night-time comings and goings.

Ask yourself why he is perpetuating this behaviour. Does he do it when the family goes away for the night? What happens when he goes away without you?

If you are convinced that sleeping in your bed has merely become routine, it should be relatively easy to change the pattern, providing you remain firm.

If, however, you consider that there are underlying emotional issues causing the child to feel insecure when away from you, then these need to be addressed.

Computer

Nowadays most homes have one or more computers which, when used appropriately, are a valuable resource for learning. However, you have a responsibility to implement basic safety principles, as well as rules about how your child uses the computer.

Possible issues may be:

- One child is dominating the use of the computer and other siblings are demanding time on it.
- Your own need for the computer is having to be tempered.
- Your child is spending so much time on the computer that he seems to be withdrawing from his family and friends.
- You may not approve of the games he is choosing to play.
- You may be worrying about his accessing chat rooms or other internet facilities.

The media regularly feature stories in which children have suffered through the misuse of computers and your fears are well founded, although possibly a little extreme. Doing nothing is not an option, for the more adept the child becomes with technology, the greater the risk.

It is a good idea to rethink the location of the computer. If it can be accessed from behind a closed door, consider moving it into a public place, such as the landing or a corner in a communal room, so you can oversee what is going on without obviously invading his space. Any new rules should address the following:

Time spent

By restricting the time you will help the child to establish his priorities: *I can see that you have become very good on the computer, but I am going to have to set a time limit on how much you use it because I think that you should also spend time doing other things when you come home from school.*

Or: *Your brother/sister wants to spend time on it too and they can't get a turn.*

Or: *I have things which I need to do on the computer and they can't always wait until you go to bed.*

Computer games

If you bought the game, you are perceived to have given it your approval. Suddenly announcing that all computer games are a waste of time is not the way forward. Instead you should aim to broaden his game-playing horizons: *I know that you enjoy playing . . . Do you always have to start it at the lowest level or could you start at a harder level and try to go further? What other games do you enjoy? Have you played them recently? What else can you do on the computer? What sort of things do you use it for at school?*

Internet access

You can put limits on this by barring access to certain sites. The reasons should be discussed with him or he will think that you do not trust him: *The internet is a vast area of information and no one checks what is available on all of the sites. To make the best use of it we need to limit ourselves to what is useful to us and also to what is suitable for your age. I am worried that some of the sites might contain information or pictures which could upset you and so I have set the computer up to protect you from these sites. It will not stop you from looking up the things which you are interested in.*

When talking about chat rooms you need to be absolutely clear about what you will allow your child to do. Some of his friends may have access to them. You could say: *Chat rooms have been set up so that people can talk to each other without actually seeing the other person. This worries me because some people who visit the chat rooms may not actually be the kind of person they say they are. For instance, it is very easy to pretend to be one age but actually be another age. Some very sad and lonely people use chat rooms to try to make friends. In some cases children have gone to meet a new friend from a chat room and they have found that the friend who they thought was 14 actually turned out to be a man of 40.*

You need to be clear about what rules you are going to establish. If the child is not to access chat rooms, say: *I do not want you to run the risk of meeting up with one of these sad people, even in a chat room. It is very easy to give them information which they should not know about. So you are not allowed to visit chat rooms.*

If your child takes issue with this you will need to revisit your reasons, but you should avoid using terror tactics. Ask him why he wants to meet new friends when he already has school friends. Suggest that he uses the computer to talk to known friends rather than to someone who may be completely different from what they seem.

As your child responds to the house rules, do compliment him and take some time to sit with him in order to observe his developing skills. You may well be surprised! Being involved with what he uses the computer for will place you in a better position to monitor what is happening.

Finishing what you have started

Once the initial enthusiasm for a project has passed, children often want to move on to something new before the task is complete. This might be because it is too large, not specific enough or just too difficult. If the job is to be seen through, you will need to become involved. Ask yourself if you have allowed him enough time or chosen an appropriate moment to introduce it, or whether it is simply proving to be too challenging for his current ability and powers of concentration.

If he has merely become bored, a short break should refresh him. If he is finding it difficult to move forward, you could discuss the sticking point with him: *Right, let's have a look at what the problem is together.* Give him enough assistance to enable him to take the next step alone. This will boost his confidence. If he is becoming too upset to carry on, put the job to one side, but say when you will return to it. Do not take the job over completely. This will teach him the wrong lesson, which is that he can give up at the first hurdle. Jobs which fall well within his capability should always be completed by him, even if you need to offer a little well-timed support.

If the task was sent home from school and you detect that there is a genuine problem about the teacher's expectation for your child to complete the task unaided, let the teacher know that your child was out of his depth. In so doing you are giving the teacher valuable feedback.

Food

Right from his earliest days you should avoid situations where your child is able to draw attention to himself through contentious food-related issues. It will help if you:

- Have set mealtimes, at a table, with others present, which are pleasant social occasions.
- Serve everyone with the same basic meal.
- Make it well known that the statement, 'I've never had it so I

don't like it', is not a good enough reason for not trying something.

- Manage the size of the portion so as not to overwhelm him.
- Do not allow him to have a pudding if he has barely touched the first course.
- Cut out eating between meals, especially as the mealtime approaches.

There are well-documented food problems which can develop in relatively young children. Professional help should be sought with managing them.

Going out alone

Parents want to protect their child from external danger, but at the same time it is important to recognize that he should not be denied suitable opportunities to take responsibility. If he has raised this topic with you, he has begun to feel confident enough to branch out on his own.

If you really feel that the child's request is inappropriate, you must say so, but explain why: *There is a busy road to cross and the cars travel very quickly at that point, so I cannot let you take that risk yet.*

However, you could set up a different scenario so that he can take an intermediate step towards becoming more independent: *I'll come to show you across the road and you can go on to the shop yourself. I'll wait for you to come back to where I leave you and I'll check the traffic again for you.*

If you feel that the project is probably safe, agree, but say that if he is not back by a certain time, you will have to come and look for him. Make sure that he has the means to know what the time is.

If he wants to visit a local friend for a longer visit, you might telephone the parent to tell them that he is leaving, and ask them to telephone you when he arrives. A similar arrangement for the return journey is a good idea. This gives you peace of mind and reminds him that he must not dawdle along the way.

Once he has begun to undertake independent trips, more and more requests will follow, and he will ask that the boundaries be extended. Always be quite sure that you know where he is going and who with, and tell him exactly when he has to be home. Even five minutes after the appointed time is not acceptable without a telephone call to tell you that there is some justifiable delay. Infringements should be discussed and result in some penalty. The child must realize that you mean what you say. You should not be afraid to set boundaries. Many young people express regret that their parents did not seem to care enough about what they did, or where they went, when they were children.

Stranger danger

There are two schools of thought about whether or not you should discuss this with your child. One view is that in doing so you may add to your child's anxieties and prevent him from seeking help, were he to find himself in need of assistance. The other is that children need to be made aware of the risks so that they know how to react in a threatening situation.

What you can do is:

- Tell a young child what a stranger is – someone we do not know well but who looks like an ordinary person.
- Talk about the kind of situations when a child should seek help – if he is asked to do something without his parents' permission or to go somewhere alone with an adult or to keep 'special secrets'.
- Agree, and practise, a safety plan.
- Assure him that you will always believe what he tells you and that you will do everything you can to resolve any problem. All he needs to do is to tell you when he feels that something is not right or when something makes him feel uncomfortable.
- Develop his confidence so that he can shout 'No' if he is asked to go somewhere with an adult, and tell him that he should always run away from the threat of danger.
- Locate suitable safe places, which could be used as a refuge if he gets separated from you or needs somewhere to go if he perceives that he might be in danger.
- Make sure that you know where he is at all times. He should get into the habit of checking with you before he goes off alone.

Road safety

The statistics relating to in-car child fatality, or serious accident, are a major cause for concern. It is essential to have a correctly fitted child seat for your child on every car journey, and that you insist that the straps are fastened before you set off.

Once your child is able to walk unaided you should begin to raise his awareness of road safety. For a child under 6, basic good practice includes:

- Holding an adult's hand and staying close beside you on the side away from the traffic flow.
- Watching out for entrances which would mean that a vehicle might need to cross the pavement.
- Being told that he must not cross the road alone.
- Teaching him the Green Cross Code.

Older children are better able to recognize danger, but they still need to be reminded about good road safety behaviour, especially when going out alone, or with friends. Young people between the ages of 11 and 15 are more likely to be killed, or seriously injured, as a pedestrian or cyclist than any other age group.

Young cyclists need to:

- Concentrate on other road users as well as themselves.
- Learn how to judge speed and distance.
- Maintain their bike in good condition and comply with the law concerning lights.
- Wear a correctly fitting helmet and an item of reflective clothing.
- Use cycle routes wherever possible.

Homework

Homework is a family issue, and younger children need help and encouragement to complete it. Establishing a routine early on will pay dividends later when the child needs to be self-motivated.

Teachers will give advice as to what is a suitable amount of time to be spent on homework. Stick to the guidelines; trying to embark on extended, parent-driven ses-sions may well prove to be counter-productive in the long run. If homework becomes an issue, you should deal with it swiftly by establishing the cause of the problem. Likely suspects are:

- The homework is too difficult for the child to tackle without help.
- It may not be interesting enough to stimulate his interest.
- No one else in the family has homework to do.
- There are other things which the child would prefer to be doing.
- He is too tired to apply himself.
- He could be using the issue of homework to divert attention on to himself.
- He cannot apply himself to the matter in hand because of distractions.

The problem may be the result of a combination of issues and you will need to have a discussion with him in order to try to sort out which aspects need addressing first: *Does everyone get the same homework from Mrs Bloggs?* If not, you can establish what homework everyone else is getting and why it varies. It would be better to talk to the teacher about this. Your child's homework is intended to support his learning and should serve to reinforce what is going on in school, or to prepare him for new work to follow. The teacher's answer will tell you where your child needs support. By giving appropriate assistance you may well find that some of the problems disappear.

If this approach does not help, you can say: *We need to make a special time, and place, for you to do your homework. Have you any ideas?*

He may not think any time is best or his suggestion may not match your own conviction, in which case you should move towards establishing an agreed routine. If the task is reading, a good time to do it is when he is ready for bed, perhaps including it in the bedtime story. If this does not fit in with family life, it might be done soon after getting home, but not before he has had a snack and some time to relax. Homework which requires research, or includes written tasks, should be done well before bedtime. Distractions such as the television, computer or siblings should not be close by.

If he tells you that he wants to watch a programme before doing homework, you have a choice. If you allow television to precede homework even once, you have reduced your authority for any future similar requests. It may be possible for you to record the programme for viewing later, or you can say that the homework has to be done first. Point out that the quicker the homework is done, the more likely it is that at least some of the programme may be viewed. The best situation is one where you have anticipated the viewing request and made sure that the homework has already been done. Whatever you decide (and it should be your decision), you must stick to it.

Lies, telling the truth and making excuses

Telling lies and making excuses for behaviour which has caused offence, upset or disappointment, is a normal part of growing up. You should make quite sure that your child is aware that there will be consequences if you discover that he is deliberately not telling, or is withholding, the truth, either at home or anywhere else.

You should always tell him as much of the truth as you can, and never lie to him. If you cannot tell him everything, say so: *I am sorry but there are things I cannot tell you today. I will tell you as soon as I can.* If the culture of the home is firmly grounded in telling the truth, your child will follow suit.

Dealing with blatant lies

The easiest lies to deal with are the ones which are blatant. Make it clear that you know that what he is saying is not true and ask him why he feels that he needs to lie. For instance, if he has damaged something, but denied it, you could say: *I know that is not true because . . .* (explain why). *What upsets me much more is that you decided not to tell me the truth. Why did you do that? You know it makes me much angrier if you lie, than I would be about . . .* (whatever it is he has lied about).

Help him by modelling what he should have said: *What you should have said is, yes, I did break the toy. I was really angry because Freddie kept interrupting and I wanted to get him to go away.*

When he is calm enough to listen you should talk about what must now happen to put things right. You could say: *First of all I want you to apologize to me for telling me a lie.* Wait for a genuine apology. When you get it say: *Thank you. I can see that you are as upset as I am about telling the lie. I am sure that you won't want to feel like this again, will you? Now I want to talk to you about what you should have done about Freddie instead of breaking his toy.*

The best outcome here would be that your child agrees that he should have come to you to ask for assistance in distracting Freddie. If it is realistic, he could be asked to make some gesture of recompense – trying to mend the broken object or using some pocket money towards replacing it. In this way he will realize that, in telling a lie, he has made the situation worse than it might have been. You will also be helping him to develop strategies for dealing with difficult situations.

Addressing untruths

A more difficult situation is when it only becomes clear some time after the lie that it was an untruth. You need to address this because the child must realize that you will never tolerate his telling lies, and the fact that he has perpetuated the lie makes it even worse.

Make time to talk the situation through. Your child has not become a hardened criminal merely because he has told, and lived with, a lie. There is a reason why he did it and you need to find out what it is. Remember that owning up is one of the hardest things to do, particularly if one knows that lengthy recriminations are sure to follow.

Start off by saying: *I hoped that I would never need to have this kind of conversation with you, but it seems that now we must. How do you think I am feeling at the moment?* Your child's answer and mood will tell you whether he realizes the severity of the situation. You can also ask him how he feels about the situation.

If you are satisfied that he is showing sufficient remorse, you can start putting the situation right as you would for a readily detected lie. If he seems unmoved by your opening comment, you will need to develop your theme: *Since you do not seem to be aware of just how much you have let yourself down by telling this lie* (or behaving in this way), *and by keeping it going for so long, I am going to tell you. Up to now I have always felt that we had a good understanding about the importance of telling the truth. You know that I would help you to put things right when you have done something wrong or got into trouble, but you also know that I consider telling lies to be one of the worst things you can do to those who you love and who love you. Why did you do it?*

If the child owns up immediately, he should be commended for this and the original fault should be dealt with promptly and swiftly.

If you are still not getting the answer you need, leave him alone to reflect on his actions. Tell him that you are going to come back in half an hour and that during that time he must sit and think about what has happened. Explain that it is not a time for him to play, listen to music or to do anything which stops him thinking about how to put matters right. Indicate that if he feels sorry before the stated time has elapsed he can come and find you. If you remain in the room during apparent stalemate, the situation is likely to deteriorate into one of anger, which must be avoided, because it will complicate the reconciliation.

Return after the appointed time has passed. If your child wants to move forward you will get the desired response. If not, it is time to indicate that there is to be a loss of a privilege. Say what it will be and keep to it. Any subsequent apology should not result in the reinstatement of the privilege because that will only weaken your position when you next find yourself needing to talk to your child in this way.

Manners

Parents need to be very clear about what the household expectations are in terms of good manners. Eventually your child may come to realize that his family's code of behaviour is different from that of his friends, but he should still subscribe to it at all times.

What kind of manners should you expect? These will be specific to your household, but the following are basic examples for a young child:

- Saying please and thank you.
- Eating – using appropriate utensils, closing mouth when chewing, not talking when mouth is full, making some comment about how much they enjoyed the meal and asking to leave the table.
- Conversation – listening and waiting for your turn to speak.
- Meeting and greeting – saying hello and goodbye while looking the person in the eye.
- Visiting other people's homes – behaving as you would at home and saying thank you on leaving.
- Public places – using an appropriate voice for the location, not charging round, staying close to the adult and respecting the expectations of the location, e.g. a doctor's surgery, library, etc.

Mobile phones

There is no doubt that parents find peace of mind in knowing that their child can be contacted should the need arise.

While you are likely to consider the mobile phone as little more than a vehicle for communication, your child may well have other views. There is huge credibility in owning one, and for many children it must be the right model, with all the latest facilities. Rules are needed about the choice of phone and how it is used, or you will rapidly discover that this can become a cause of family arguments. For instance, you may well find that he asks for an upgrade on a very regular basis. Alternatively, you could find that the bill is mounting up or that top-ups are needed more and more frequently.

To avoid these problems, include the child in the choice of phone and explain the call and text charges to him at the time of purchase. It is unrealistic to provide him with a mobile phone and not expect him to use it for the purpose of texting or speaking to friends. If he gets pocket money, some of this could be set aside for mobile phone costs, over and above his basic allowance. Agree the time when you will consider an upgrade and tell him not to ask about one before that date because you will not agree to any change ahead of schedule. Explain to him that misuse of the phone will not be tolerated and will result in its withdrawal. Misuse means infringing any school rules which relate to mobiles, any inappropriate use such as bullying by text messaging and running up bills, without prior agreement, which are in excess of the agreed amount and which the child cannot fund from his pocket money.

You should monitor the cost of the phone and compliment him if it is within bounds. This will indicate that you are remaining vigilant about the costs. Consider changing the way the phone is paid for if call and text patterns suggest that you could get a better deal.

Noise

Noise made by someone else, when you want peace and quiet, can become a major irritant and children can make a lot of noise when they are playing, feeling angry, or even listening to music or watching television, to name just a few examples.

If you are finding the noise level excessive you need to tell him that his noise is too loud because, for instance, you cannot hear the radio in the kitchen. A sound level check such as this will help him to put his noise into a context. If the noise level rises again, ask him to change his activity because he cannot seem to undertake it within an acceptable level of noise.

Listening to music becomes more important to children as they get older. It is the basis of much social interaction and it would be unreasonable to stop it altogether. There is nothing to be gained from making subjective comments about the quality of the music; but guidance is needed as to how loud it should be and when it can be listened to. Headphones can be a good idea, but volume control should be monitored in order to avoid permanent damage to the ears. Periodically you should ask your child if you can listen to his headphones and make a comment about the volume: *I am glad you are being careful about your ears. I know of too many people who have poor hearing because they listened to lots of very loud music when they were younger.* Or: *The music sounds good loud but you must limit how much time you listen to it as loud as this or else you will have problems with your hearing when you are older.*

Some children can manage to do their homework very successfully while listening to music, but others may find it too distracting. Observe the effect music has on your child and agree a listening programme which works well for him.

Parents' time out

All parents need time to themselves, and children can benefit from a well-managed break from their parents.

As a child gets older he may bring pressure to bear prior to the separation, particularly if he feels excluded and the adults' outing sounds fun. This can be avoided if the time out is seen as a normal part of family life, the surrogate carer is chosen carefully and the child's arrangements are presented in a positive way.

If your child is of an age to understand, tell him exactly what you are doing and when you will be back and who is looking after him. Leave swiftly and do not indulge in lingering goodbyes. Make sure you leave contact details and say when you will be back. Do not extend your absence without due cause or without ringing to explain.

Longer trips need to be prepared for in more detail, but the principles are the same. A short telephone call in order to maintain contact can be useful, but if you think it will unsettle the child, don't make it when he is around. If you've told him that you will telephone, do so. On your return, ask him what he most enjoyed about his experience. Tell him about yours, but be certain to say how nice it is to come home to such a cheerful person. He will appreciate a small gift but do not present it as a reward for good behaviour. Instead, tell him that you thought he would like something to remind him of the time so-and-so looked after him.

Pet care

Many children yearn for a pet at some point. Before welcoming one into the household you need to remind everyone of the old adage that a pet is not just for Christmas, because pets are both time-consuming and expensive.

Before you agree to a pet, discuss what type of animal it should be. Explain why you cannot have a dog if that is your view and stress the benefits of owning the particular type of pet you are prepared to bring into the home. Go into some detail about what the pet will need in terms of care: cleaning out its quarters, a feeding regime, an exercise programme, socialization, etc. Obtain a commitment from your child in terms of looking after it. Remind him that the pet could live for several years and that his contribution to it must last as long as he lives at home. Say what your part will be because you will need to be involved too.

Once the pet's novelty value has passed, the child may be less inclined to feed it, water it or exercise it. If so, remind him of his commitment and show him that you have stuck to your word and are still doing what you promised to. Ask him why he has a problem with his role. It could be that there is a justifiable cause and if so you may need to redefine his contribution, but he must still continue to take an active part in caring for the pet. If you allow him not to keep his promise, he will learn that commitment and responsibility can be shirked.

If care of the pet continues to be an issue, you could introduce a weekly chart which allows you to rotate duties.

Pocket money

This issue needs clarification from the moment it has been decided that the child is to receive it. Exactly what it is for, how much is being given, and how often, must be spelt out, leaving no room for misunderstanding. If, for instance, you want him to save some of it or to spend some on presents at Christmas and/or family birthdays, you must explain this and arrange for him to save money in such a way that he can see it accumulating. It is a good idea to explain the principle of earning interest to an older child, so that he learns the value of keeping money in a safe place, over time.

If you decide to give him total freedom over what he spends his money on, you should be prepared for him to want to buy sweets and consumables which you may not necessarily feel represent value for money. Having decided to give him complete freedom, it is probably too late to start laying down guidelines.

Once the child becomes used to having an income, some controversial money-related issues may arise.

Unfavourable comparisons with siblings or peers

You may well be told that all his friends get more pocket money than he does, or that his friends don't have to spend theirs on gifts for other people or save any of it. This may well be true. If you are not interested in comparisons with other children, you must say so, and tell him why. For instance, you may be subsidizing your child's spending more than other parents do, or you may not want to give him more because of your own financial circumstances. Your reasons are valid and if you explain he should accept them. If you can afford to be more flexible, you may decide to talk to the parents of other children to gather some information about the going rate and terms. Should this result in your deciding to give more, or to relax the criteria, say that you will review the matter after a specific time, and not before, so that he does not gain the impression that every time he creates a fuss you will increase his pocket money.

Running out of money ahead of pay day

Ask him what he needs the money for now, and why he cannot wait until pocket-money day. If you decide that he has a genuine need, you could consider making him an advance payment which will be deducted from the next allocation, or you could meet the cost yourself. If, however, you think that he should have budgeted more carefully, tell him that he will have to wait until pay day. Do not allow him to take it from his savings.

Wanting to use saved money for items other than the agreed criteria

This is an opportunity to discuss wider money-related issues, such as the value of budgeting and prioritizing. Again, find out what he feels he needs, which he cannot afford out of his current assets. Unless you can see that the item will make a significant, and hopefully long-term, contribution to your child's life, he should be told to wait and save hard for the item.

Presents

Everyone loves to receive, and children need to be shown not only how to be a grateful recipient, but also that there is much pleasure to be gained from giving.

There are episodes in a child's life when he will receive presents – birthdays and religious festivals being the most obvious. On such occasions the number and size of the gifts can become the focus of his attention.

It is a good idea to pace the present opening so that attention is focused on each one, separately. Tell him that, as there are lots of presents, he is going to open them slowly, one at a time, so that the enjoyment lasts as long as possible. Encourage him to investigate each gift carefully and to say why he is pleased with it.

There will be inevitable disappointments when the contents do not live up to his expectations. At such times you should point out how kind the donor is.

Children should write thank-you letters. This can cause grumbles, but the letter does not need to be a lengthy piece of prose, and he needs to learn that it is appropriate to say thank you when he has been given something.

Children also need to learn that there will be times when others receive a present and they do not. This can be very hard for a young child and it is always helpful to explain it in advance. Involve him in the giving process if you can, even if it is merely handing over the present. Some children find it impossible to keep the contents of a present from the eventual recipient, so do not tell or show him what is inside if this is likely to put him under pressure.

Rewards and punishment

The key to successful behaviour management lies in giving a child constant feedback. Always praise the positive, no matter how small it seems to you, because your child will grow in confidence. By ignoring minor infringements your child will come to understand that there is nothing to be gained from perpetuating this particular behaviour.

Reward systems work, but only if the child respects the reward, knows that you do too, and if everyone sticks to the rules. Rewards should accumulate and the target should be something to which he can really look forward, or the effect will decrease very quickly.

A reward system is best used to modify specific aspects of negative behaviour. Tidying the bedroom is too broad a task and it does not have a time frame. Making his bed each morning is both achievable and quantifiable.

The format of the reward system should be clearly set against the desired behaviour. A star chart, with one star or smiley face for each positive outcome is a good starting point, but once an agreed time has passed, this should be set aside with some positive conclusion such as: *Now you have finished the chart we will go to the cinema because we are very pleased that you have shown that you can go to bed sensibly each evening. Since you know that it makes us so pleased I know that you will carry on doing it for us.*

If you want to reduce stress at bedtime, first decide how you think this might best be achieved. Your child can only fully respond to one reward system at a time and so you should target the behaviour which you wish to modify. A chart might look something like the one in Table 1.

Table 1 An example of a reward chart

	Mon.	Tues.	Wed.	Thurs.	Fri.	Sat.	Sun.
Switching the TV off when asked							
Having a bath in less than 15 minutes							
Turning the light off by 8.30 p.m.							

The next stage is to discuss this with your child: *We are all finding bedtime difficult and it should be a nice end to the day. I have made this chart for us. This is how it will work. If you manage to do what it says, we will put a smiley face in the box. If not, the box stays empty. At the end of the week if you get more than * smileys* (*decide on a realistic number which should not reflect 100 per cent success – this is unlikely and failure will result in more negative behaviour and the feeling that there is no point in trying to achieve success) *we will go to the cinema.*

At the end of the week your child's chart may look something like the one in Table 2. It should be discussed carefully with the child: *Monday and Saturday were the best days. You were fantastic on those days and you have got so much better at putting the light out now. I am really pleased with that. The one thing which is not as good as the rest is switching off the TV. Next week we will work especially hard on this, as well as the rest.*

The chart should be repeated for another week and comparisons discussed with your child. Things should be better. If not, then no outing to the cinema, and significant disappointment should be shown: *I am really disappointed. I thought you had decided to show us how responsible you had become about going to bed, but this week has* *been worse than last. I was planning to stop the chart but now we will do it again next week and you must get * smileys* (*this total must be more than the first week but not by too many) *to show us that you are really trying to please us.*

Table 2 How a completed reward chart might look

	Mon.	*Tues.*	*Wed.*	*Thurs.*	*Fri.*	*Sat.*	*Sun.*
Switching the TV off when asked	☺		☺	☺		☺	
Having a bath in less than 15 minutes	☺	☺			☺	☺	☺
Turning the light off by 8.30 p.m.	☺	☺	☺		☺	☺	☺

You will need to really help the child to succeed during this week. It will be important for future reward schemes. Success breeds success.

Finally, think very carefully before deciding to reward children with money because how much you give the first time will become a benchmark for the future, and your child is likely to try to raise the stakes.

The opposite of reward is punishment. Empty boxes on a chart tell the child that you are not pleased and everyone else can see them too, which is very effective. Try very hard not to have too many or the situation becomes a no-win one for you, or your child. Sending him to bed even earlier because he has not met the set criteria would be counter-productive because bedtime would return to being a time of conflict, which is the very thing you are trying to avoid.

The best approach is to tell him why you are very disappointed with what has happened or with what he has not done. Do this immediately and then move on positively.

If you feel that more is needed by way of punishment, withdrawing something he enjoys should work. Avoid sending him to his room because this can result in his bedroom becoming a negative space rather than a pleasant place in which to spend time: *Because I am upset that you keep on shouting at me, I have decided that you cannot watch TV this evening. I am unhappy because you shout at me and I want you to understand what it feels like to be made to feel unhappy by someone else.*

Physical punishment is never the answer. It may make you feel better initially, but ultimately no one benefits. You will have to work hard to overcome the damage done (emotional as well as physical) to your child, and in hitting him you are seen as a role model who condones inappropriate physical behaviour. Your child may well start to reflect your behaviour with his siblings and peers.

Shopping

Your child is unlikely to be excited by the prospect of a shopping trip unless you are going out with the express intention of buying him something. So, you need to make it absolutely clear that you *may* purchase something for him *if* you are planning to, but if not, you must say so. Resorting to a bribe: *If you are good I'll get you a . . .* only sets up a cause and effect expectation, which can get out of hand on future shopping expeditions.

It will help if you lay down the ground rules before you set out: *We are going to the supermarket to buy all the things we need for the next few days and then we will be going to the park this afternoon. It won't take long to do the shopping if we can find everything quickly. You can help me look for the dog food.*

Or: *It is ages since we went into town. I need a new pair of shoes and so we will have to look in a few shops. We can have a drink when we have found the shoes.*

Or: *It is your birthday next week and so we are going to look for something very special for you. We might find it today, but we might not. We will need to be careful that we don't just buy the first thing you like because we might see something even better later on. I will need to tell you whether I have enough money for the things you like. If I can't afford them, we will keep looking.*

Once the trip is under way, stick to the brief and keep commending your child's positive behaviour. Include him as much as possible. *Shall we have strawberry yoghurts today? Do you like these shoes, or those?*

Carry out your promise of going to the park, having a drink, etc. When you get home tell him how much you enjoyed shopping with him. After all, you'll be making many future trips!

Stealing

If your child has stolen something it may mean that he felt that he could not obtain it through other more conventional methods, or that he thought that you would not give your consent if he asked for it.

If he is to learn from his mistakes you will need an action plan. The first thing to consider is his age. The next is whether or not this has happened before. If a pattern of stealing is emerging, your child has learnt that this method of obtaining something is easier than having to ask for it, wait for it or pay for it, and that detection does not necessarily follow. Where he has been found out previously, any resulting punishment has not acted as a sufficient deterrent. The object(s) which have been stolen are of lesser significance at this stage; it is the act of taking something which does not belong to him, and giving it back, which you need to focus on.

The young child

The first time you find something in his pocket, book bag or somewhere else, which you know is not his, you must remain calm. If it has come home from school,merely say: *This belongs to Mrs Bloggs, doesn't it? We will take it back tomorrow and explain that you brought it home by mistake.* Give it back to the teacher in front of your child but keep it very low key. The very young child will not have consciously stolen the object, he or she just wanted to have it for now. If you are not sure whose it is, say: *I haven't seen this before. Who does it belong to? Does she know you have got it?*

Mrs Bloggs is quite unlikely to have given your child a toy or similar object to take home, and keep, without telling you, but a friend may have done, so you need to be careful about coming straight out with an accusation. You can say: *I think I had better ask Jennifer if she is sure that you can keep it, because she may want it back.* Knowing your child as you do, you will be able to tell straight away, from his body language, if things are not open and above board. If you are suspicious say: *I tell you what, we'll give it back to her at the school gate tomorrow morning. I'll tell her that you made a mistake and that we both wanted her to have it back as soon as possible.* Take possession of the object and close the matter. The next morning remind your child that you will be giving Jennifer her item back and make sure that he is present at the handover.

If the situation arises again, you should say that the act of taking something which does not belong to you is not allowed. You can say that we call it stealing and that people get into a lot of trouble if they steal, so your child must not start doing it. You can say that now that he knows that it is not allowed by anyone, you know that he won't take anything that does not belong to him again.

Each time you find something which has been wrongly acquired you need to involve your child in giving it back. If it is becoming a regular problem you need to make this quite difficult for him by taking less and less of a moderate view and saying: *I have helped you before when we gave Jennifer her toy back, but now you are going to have to decide what to say to Mark.*

You need to give some thought as to why he is stealing and what it is you are finding. Discuss this with him. You may find that there are things which he wants, which will give him status within the peer group, or he may be taking money, or food. Whatever it is, he perceives that he has a need for it. Say: *In future, please tell me if there is something you think you need, and we will talk about it.* It would not be right to merely reward the stealing by immediately giving him more pocket money if he asks for it, or by taking him out and buying the desired object, but you may decide that he does actually need more pocket money or to take a snack to school. After a few days you can say: *I have thought about your pocket money and I am going to give you * amount more each week, starting next week.* (Having to wait a little while will indicate that you are still in charge.) *If you want to buy something special with it let me know and I'll make sure that you can go into town, when you have saved enough money, to get it.*

The older child

Older children know that they have taken something which is not theirs and should be well acquainted with the concept of theft. Your attitude should be one of zero-tolerance, but if it is the first offence you should be helpful in rectifying the situation, much as with the younger child. If stealing has become a habit you need to tell the child a few home truths:

1 That you consider all stealing to be very wrong.
2 That you will never, ever, consider that stealing happens by mistake.
3 That the person who steals is the one who has done wrong, even if they were encouraged to do it by someone else.
4 That stealing is always taken very seriously at school and by the police, and that people must be punished for what is considered to be a crime.
5 That you will never do anything dishonest, like lying, to protect your child.
6 That you are there to help your child break the habit, but if the stealing is going on at school you will need to cooperate with the school, or newsagent, or whoever has been the victim of the theft, in order to put it right. If it involves friends or other people, tell your child that you will need to talk to the people concerned about what he has done.

This will not be an easy conversation, but it must take place. The next step is for you to ask him about the situations which prompt him to steal. Asking *why* he steals is too big an issue for him to answer specifically. Say: *Are there times when you feel that you can steal something without getting found out?* If there are, and possibilities could be in the cloakroom at break, or in the newsagent's after school, make a plan with him which will enable him to avoid finding himself in the vulnerable situation. Asking him how he feels when he knows he has done wrong is not likely to elicit the required answer, especially if he is stealing in the company of friends. A better question is: *Do you think I will carry on helping you to put things right for ever? What do you think might happen if the police find out about this?* The child needs to understand the severity of the situation and that you are not there to prevent him from taking responsibility for his own actions. He should also make suitable recompense to the person he has stolen from. You should decide what this is to be. It should involve some significant input from the child, and could be financial or practical in nature.

Sweets

Many of us enjoy sweet things and children are generally no exception. Sweets can be offered as an occasional treat, or as a reward, or they can be withdrawn as a punishment. *I am so pleased with the bedtime chart that I am going to take you to the newsagent's for a treat after school on Monday. You can buy* (something of his choice). Or: *Because I was disappointed with the number of smileys on the chart we will not be going to the newsagent for any sweets this week.*

Sweets should only be used as one part of the reward scheme. Varying the rewards will prove more interesting to your child and is also much healthier.

Apart from using them to reinforce positive behaviour, some parents feel that sweets provide a pleasant bonus at the weekend. If your child understands the concept of money it is essential to tell him, before he enters the shop, how much he can spend and whether or not he must share his purchases.

The same applies if he is choosing to spend his own money on sweets. It is not a good idea for him to spend all of it in this way and you should tell him what amount per week can be spent on sweets and why it needs to be limited. Stressing the benefits of other purchases will help to deflect him from the attraction of chocolate and the like.

Television

Like the computer, television can contribute a great deal to the child's world, both educationally and socially, but, if not monitored, the child can spend so much time passively in front of the screen that he misses out on other beneficial activities and he runs the risk of seeing material which is inappropriate for his age and stage of development.

Parents should decide how much viewing time is acceptable, and which programmes you consider suitable, and explain these guidelines to your child. You must stick to them. You will probably be told that his friends are allowed to watch certain programmes which you do not permit. You can say: *I am sure that some of them do, and maybe their parents don't mind them watching programmes about* (list some of the likely story lines) *but I don't want you to see that sort of thing at the moment. We can talk about this again when* (give a future time), *but for now I am not going to change my mind.*

Scrutinize the TV listings and look out for stimulating and beneficial programmes which fall outside your normal viewing agreement and record these for your child. Watching them can be a reward for something positive. This will show him that it is the act of watching anything which comes on which you find a problem, not all TV programmes.

You will need to tell the babysitter what the house rules are because your child may try to bend them if you are not around. If there are several siblings it is a good idea to differentiate their viewing profiles. It will show the older one that you recognize that he is growing up and the younger one will realize that he has the promise of more viewing as he matures.

Tidying up

There is no reason why a child cannot help with tidying up after himself. Even very young children are capable of putting toys away in a convenient container. Parents may feel that it is easier if they do it themselves, but this will only perpetuate the problem into the teenage years, when untidiness can get out of hand.

Your child needs to know that the task is achievable. This means that it needs to be broken down into small parts. Saying: *Please tidy up the playroom* is not specific enough. His view of tidiness is unlikely to be the same as yours. Instead say: *Please put all the cars away in this box. Excellent, now can you put the train set away in its container?*

In the same way you need to itemize tasks for the older child. Say: *Please bring all the washing down and put it on the floor in front of the washing machine. Thank you, now I need all the mugs brought down because we are running out of them and they need to be washed.*

Older children may regard any assistance as insulting or an intrusion into their space. Offer to help, but if they say no, respect this but tell them what aspect of the mess you need to be sorted out and by when.

Visitors and visiting

Having visitors can be a stressful experience if not managed carefully. Less preparation is needed for a short visit, but a longer one needs some planning. Visiting others should be a pleasure, and will be with suitable guidelines.

Adult visitors

The short-term visitor will probably be coming for a drink or a meal. Your child should be told who the person is – friend, business colleague, etc. – and why he or she is coming. You should tell him the arrangements and what is expected of him during the visit.

If adults are coming to stay, it may mean that your child is displaced from his bedroom and will certainly result in normal routines being set aside. Be quite clear about who is coming, for how long and where the visitor will sleep. Explain what the reason for the visit is and how it will include, or maybe exclude, the child. If the latter, you will need to make time during the visit for the child so that he does not feel completely ignored. Such feelings can result in attention-seeking behaviour of the kind which you would not want, because it could spoil the visit. When the visitors have gone, be sure to commend your child for cooperating.

Young visitors

Arranging for other children to visit your home is an important part of all children's social life. Be sure that it is your child who wants the visitor to come and not you who wants to see his or her parent, if the parent comes too. The best visits are short, spontaneous and initiated by the children themselves. They will find mutually agreeable things to do and you can leave them to it, producing refreshments as appropriate. Complex pre-planned visits can become over-hyped and turn out to be an anticlimax.

Before the child arrives, it is useful to discuss the visit: *What do you think George will want to do while he is here? What shall we have for tea? He may want to play with the train set. Are you going to set it up before he comes?* This type of discussion serves to remind your child that he is the host and as such has certain responsibilities, sharing toys being one of them. It can also be helpful if the situation later deteriorates and a quarrel develops, because you can take your child to one side and remind him that you had discussed what they were going to do and it is important that George enjoys himself.

If a child is coming to stay for a night or longer then you need to be clear about any customs which his parents would like you to do your best to comply with. This may lead to a discussion about realistic expectations, perhaps about diet or bathing. Do not make promises which you cannot keep, but respect their values, as you would wish them to do the same in return. Once the child has arrived you need to talk to all the children concerned about how the visit is to be spent, what rules will be adhered to and what the visiting child should do if he needs help at any time.

Older children will want to spend a lot of time closeted away in the bedroom. This is fine, but visit them from time to time to suggest distractions.

When your child is invited to other homes, be sure that he really wants to go. Remind him of his manners. If a meal is involved, tell him what to say if there is something he does not like to eat: *I am afraid I don't like sausages.* Tell him when you will be collecting him and be prompt. If he is to stay the night be very careful to explain what you have agreed with the parents as to bedtime, etc. and tell him how he can make contact with you if he really feels that he needs to. Allow him to choose most of what he needs to take and a young child should take a favourite bedtime toy.

2

Milestones

Introduction

Life consists of a series of milestones which start in early childhood. Children need to be prepared for significant events so that their expectations are realistic. If a young child's imagination is allowed free rein she is likely to experience a sense of anticlimax when the reality fails to match her anticipation. Older children need to be given factual information, in good time, so that they are well prepared for the significant events which they will face.

New baby

The expectation of a new baby will inevitably alter the dynamics of family life because during the pregnancy the adults concerned will naturally become more focused on the impending birth. Every effort should be made to ensure that any siblings fully understand what is going to happen. However, very young children find the concept of passing time difficult to grasp, particularly if it is more than a few days, and telling them that they are to have a new brother or sister in seven months, or so, is not going to be particularly helpful because they will think that it is far more imminent than it really is.

By the time that the new baby is due you should have discussed the following:

- What will happen to any siblings during labour and its immediate aftermath.
- How long you expect to be in hospital.
- Whether anyone else is coming to help out during the period surrounding the birth.
- Whether the new baby is a boy or a girl (if you know) and which names you are considering.

A younger child will need to know about:

- The practical arrangements you are making: sleeping arrangements, etc.
- What the new baby will require in terms of care – lots of feeding, nappy changing, bathing, etc. – and which aspects of these the sibling can help with.
- What the new baby will be able to do, and more significantly what he or she will not be able to do – sit up, play with the sibling, focus on the sibling, etc.

Older siblings may become interested in how the baby was conceived.

Whatever the age of the sibling it is essential that time is set aside for her to receive your undivided attention, both during the pregnancy and in the immediate aftermath of the birth. Explaining that it is hard work having a new baby in the family and telling her that you would find it very difficult if she were not there, for instance, at the baby's bath time, will be invaluable in helping her to come to terms with the new arrival.

If there seems to be some resentment towards the new arrival, you need to establish the basis for this. Observe the older sibling carefully to see when she appears jealous. It may be when the baby is being bathed, or is feeding. These are the times when you will need to involve her. You should also watch out for how she reveals her jealousy. If she tries to hurt the baby, you will need to talk about this in a very gentle way, stressing how vulnerable the baby is. If she becomes angry or withdrawn, you need to tell her that you understand how she feels, because everything is different now that the baby is here, but that this is how the family is now and you all need to think about the good things which having a new baby brings to the family.

Birthdays

Difficulties are likely to arise if other children in the family become jealous of the birthday child, if presents do not fulfil expectations or if the child wishes to celebrate her birthday in a way which you disapprove of, or cannot cater for.

Where there are other children, you will need to establish an understanding that birthdays are the one day every year when each of us should be made to feel particularly special: *I can remember very clearly the day you were born.* (Young children are fascinated by this concept – they find it amazing that there was life before their birth.) *It was a very special day and still is. I was so thrilled when you finally arrived because I had been waiting for you for a very long time. Later I decided that every year I would make everyone's birthday a very special day.*

If it is a sibling's birthday you can say: *We are getting ready to celebrate* (name)'s *birthday and now you are old enough to help me to make it a great day for him/her. When it is your birthday I will make sure that you have a special day too. What do you think we should do to make it special?*

If your child wishes to mark her birthday in a way that you cannot condone or afford, make this clear right from the outset: *I can see that you would like to have a disco/go to the burger bar/go to see a film, but I am afraid that I do not think this is a suitable thing to do on your own this year. In a year or two, yes, but now, no.* Or: *Taking everyone out for a meal is too expensive. I cannot afford it.*

Be ready to suggest alternative strategies: *How about everyone comes here and we have a pizza making party?* Or: *We can arrange a trip to the cinema for you and four friends. I'll take you and collect you afterwards. What about having a sleepover party? We can get the room set up so that you all sleep together and I'll make some food so that you can have a late-night feast.*

Children need guidance as to how to make their parent's birthday special. All that is needed is consideration for the adult, and it may be a good idea for someone to explain this by pointing out that, for instance, tidying her bedroom without nagging would be such a bonus that it would be the best possible birthday present. If you live alone with your child it is perfectly acceptable to give her a little prompt: *It is my birthday next week. I would love it if you would do one of your beautiful drawings for me.* If appropriate you could say: *To celebrate my birthday we could go out for lunch on Saturday. I would like to go to . . .* (your favourite child-friendly restaurant).

Starting school

The day your child starts school is a significant milestone for parent and child alike. This is true whether your child is starting school for the first time or transferring between schools. It should be viewed as an exciting new opportunity because it will mean that a variety of fresh, outside influences are brought into the home, with new friendships being formed with other children, new relationships with significant adults, and changes being introduced into the domestic routine.

In all probability the school will guide you through the process. Take advantage of any opportunities it offers you and/or your child to visit, and see if it is possible to make contact with other families whose child will be in the same class as yours. Go past the school frequently and refer to it positively and regularly in your everyday conversation:

- *I can remember when I started school, I felt really grown up.*
- *I made a lot of new friends when I went to school and I used to ask them home for tea and sometimes I went to their house to play too.*
- *I had very kind teachers who showed me how to do lots of new and exciting things. I really like Mrs Bloggs and I know that she will do this too.*
- *At playtime we all went out into the playground together. It was lovely to have so many people to play with.*
- *The school lunches were delicious.*
- *While I was at school my Mummy went to work/stayed at home, etc. I will be . . .* (say what you will be doing but do not make it sound too interesting) *while you are at school.*
- *. . . . . .* (say who) *will take you to school each day and meet you when it is time to come home.*
- *I can't wait to hear about all the wonderful things you will do at school.*

You can ask your child what she enjoyed most at school that day but do not press her for an answer. School is her world and she may want to keep it separate from home life. In all likelihood she will be very tired and just need to relax back into home life at the end of a busy day.

Reading

The very young child feels enormously proud of her first steps in mastering reading and any reading tasks sent home from school should be afforded due time and attention by the parent.

- Choose the time to read together carefully. Ten minutes of quality reading time the next morning will be much more productive than half an hour in the evening when everyone is exhausted.
- There is absolutely no merit in rushing your child through the book. Reading is not just a matter of reading text and ticking off as many books as you can in the shortest possible time. If your child is to grow up loving reading, and books, you have a part to play in developing her enjoyment. This can be achieved by discussing the pictures, talking about the characters and responding to the mood which the book creates.
- Read books to her and be seen to read yourself.
- Show her that you love reading.
- Refer to books as sources of reference.

Not all children find reading easy. You may begin to notice that she avoids reading-related activities, or that she is not making what you consider to be satisfactory progress.

There are many possible reasons why this might be the case and the teacher and parent must work closely together to analyse the situation. Ask for a meeting, at a time when your child will not be present, and do not wait until the next scheduled parent/teacher meeting. Your discussion should include the following topics:

- Explain why you have called the meeting.
- Establish what the teacher feels about your child's progress. If she is reassuring, you should be guided by her. Remember that she will be able to make a professional judgement about how much progress your child has already made over time and not just in the area of reading. She will be able to compare this with the norm for your child's age group. She will also be able to explain further how children learn to read, which is different for every child.
- If there is any family history of reading difficulties, these should be shared with the teacher.

- Whatever the teacher's professional view is of your child's reading ability, she should acknowledge your concerns and agree an action plan for the next two weeks. This may include:
  - taking a reading homework holiday,
  - changing the level of difficulty and style of book which comes home. Do not discount going back to what may seem to you to be much simpler text. The child needs a boost in confidence.

During this period the teacher should establish exactly what the child can do and where any problems lie. As the parent you should agree not to bring any pressure to bear on the child, either now or later.

At the second meeting the teacher will be able to explain her findings. She will advise you about practical ways in which you can support your child, such as by playing suitable word games. Depending on the level of difficulty, you may both agree that further outside professional help is needed. See this as a positive. You will be included every step of the way and all such help is designed to support your child and assist her in making suitable progress.

It may be the case that the teacher raises the matter of your child's reading ability with you. If so, be prepared to listen and respond positively. After all, you are both motivated to help your child move forward.

Absence of a parent

There are many reasons why one or other parent will need to leave the family home, either temporarily, or as a permanent change in the family dynamics. It is quite possible that your child's behaviour may change, either subtly or more obviously. She may become more reserved or start seeking attention by being clingy or badly behaved. The teacher may report that she is not her usual self. (You should always tell the school of any changes in family circumstances which could have a bearing on the child.) Your child may talk a great deal about the absent parent. She may ask endless questions about where the other parent is and what he or she will be doing, or she may exclude the missing parent from all conversation.

She will not understand why the parent is absent unless you give her a reason. She will feel insecure because of the change in circumstances and may even feel guilty, particularly if there have been recent family arguments which she has overheard.

You will need to agree between yourselves what explanation you are going to give her. This should be based on the truth and include a time frame.

Comments like this are helpful:

- *Mum has to go away to stay with Gran because she needs to look after her for a few days. We are not sure how long she will be there, but I will let you know more when I can.*
- *Mum is quite tired at the moment and so we have decided that she should have a rest at her friend . . . . . .'s house for a while. We will be able to talk to her on the telephone after school on Friday.*
- *Dad has a lot of work to do and the people he works for have asked him to go to America. We can send him messages and photographs of us all from the computer.*

Do listen to what your child asks you about the situation and respond constructively. Never lie. If you don't know the answer, say so, but say that you will try to find it out for her.

It is always helpful to establish regular connection with the absent parent, particularly if the absence is going to be prolonged. This may appear to unsettle everyone for a short period after the contact, but it is a good investment. The child will feel reassured that the absent parent is still part of her life. It is very useful to keep the absent parent well informed about significant moments and issues for the child and for the one who is absent to refer to these in communications:

- *Mum told me all about your super assembly. I was so proud to hear how well you read your story, etc. Maybe I can ask Mrs Bloggs to let me read it when I come home.*
- *Dad tells me that you can cook buns now. I am looking forward to tasting your cooking when I come home.*
- *Mum says that you are being an enormous help to her by going to bed on time and doing your homework quickly. I am really proud of you.*

It is also helpful to the child if she is prepared for any real-time communication: *Let's make a list of the things we have to tell Daddy about when he telephones tomorrow.* (A picture list will serve as a good prompt for the very young child.)

Make a point of including the absent parent in your daily conversations. For example: *Mum really likes this dress. Do you want to wear it today?* Or: *Daddy would be able to help you with your homework. We'll tell him we are having difficulties with the French when we next speak to him.*

Divorce

However difficult it proves to be, both parents should avoid passing any related anger, guilt, or other negative emotion on to their child.

It will be very helpful if both parents can be seen to communicate with each other about child-related issues such as school-based meetings or other public events. You must avoid any situation where your child might feel that she is having to act as a go-between, or where she finds herself acting as piggy-in-the-middle. If the adults' emotions are still very raw, allocate particular events to one parent or the other and explain who will attend each one to your child. This should be made into a positive: *Daddy will want to see how the match goes against Newtown so he will be there that afternoon. I will be taking you to your swimming lessons though, so that I can see how you are getting on each week.* Make sure that the absent parent is kept up to date with the child's current interests and with significant changes or occurrences in her life. For instance, the absent parent needs to know that a particular craze has become last week's news in order to avoid the situation where the child feels that her life is becoming marginalized by the parent who lives away.

Children need to be told about how their lives will change once the parents have divorced. The implications of divorce should be explained to older children. Initial conversations should include reference to:

- The fact that the decision has been taken so as to make things less stressful for everyone.
- The fact that the child is not to blame.
- That, although there is to be a divorce, the absent parent will always be the child's parent.
- That any new adults will not replace the child's blood parents.
- That many families experience divorce, so the child need not worry about being unusual.
- The arrangements for seeing the absent parent.

A checklist of topics to discuss when an adult is leaving the home should include:

- When the person concerned will be leaving.
- Whether you consider this to be a permanent or temporary situation.
- Where the departing adult is going to live and, if applicable, with whom.
- Whether this has any immediate impact on the child's living arrangements. At this stage it is probably best not to discuss very long-term plans as they may well change. Although if asked, and you think a relocation may be on the cards, you can say: *It may be that we need to move house too in a while, but at the moment I am concentrating on getting used to things here with you. I will let you know if we will be moving when I know more.*
- What the arrangements will be for spending time with the departing adult. (Do ensure that initially this time is spent one to one with the absent parent and not with any new partner. The child may need to rebuild her relationship with the parent without any outside influences being present, and during early visits they deserve to be the centre of their absent parent's attention.)
- How the child can keep in touch with the absent parent.

If a new partner is to join your household this should not happen suddenly, without prior introduction or a period of familiarization. Instead, it should become the natural outcome after an extended period during which everyone gets to know each other well.

In this situation a checklist for conversations with your child should include:

- The benefits of having the new adult move in – practical ones are less likely to cause any emotional distress to the child: *Having John around the house makes things easier because he helps with the shopping/collecting you from parties/decorating, etc.* Avoid saying things like: *I am much happier now that John is living here.* This sends the wrong message to the child about the absent parent and should be avoided because, whatever your personal views may be, your child needs to maintain a good long-term relationship with her other parent.

- If the newcomer has family commitments of his or her own, you need to explain that on certain days these will be honoured.

The situation becomes more complex if the new arrival brings additional children to the family unit. This should only become a permanent arrangement after a lengthy period of getting to know each other, during shared outings on neutral territory, has taken place.

When combining two families you need to ensure that each child has frequent opportunities to spend quality time, free from any interference from the children of the other adult, with their own parent. This will take some planning, but it does not need to be a major production. A visit to the supermarket might suffice.

You should be prepared for a period of realignment, whereby all the children try to establish their credentials in the family pecking order. Work hard to ensure that all feel valued, have their own space and know that you love them without question. Tell them so on a regular basis.

Finally, it is worth remembering that there will be a significant number of split families in any one class at your child's school and several of your child's friends may belong to reconfigured family groups, so it is best not to make any assumptions about the composition and responsibilities of the members in a family group. If, for instance, your child's friend is coming to stay for the weekend be quite clear about who you should contact in an emergency.

Moving house

It should be remembered that, ultimately, the adults involved will have made the decision to relocate and that unless the child is kept fully informed she may experience all kinds of related uncertainties.

These anxieties could be about starting at a new school, the loss of existing friendships and, if the family group is to change permanently, there may well be territorial worries or anxieties about the absent parent and the new family members.

It will reassure your child if you indicate how you plan to keep in touch with those you will be leaving behind, and mean it: *As you know we are all very happy here but this house is too small/ I have got a new job/ we want a bigger garden and now that we have found the right house for us to live in we will be moving in about four weeks' time. In choosing the new house we have thought very carefully about your new school and the fact that you enjoy football/dancing and I have found out about the local football club. They are always keen to have new players. Your new school has a marvellous . . . and I really liked the teacher whose class you will be in. As soon as you have made some new friends we will be able to arrange for you to meet up with them out of school. I have already spoken to Joanna's mum and she has agreed that Joanna can come and stay with us during the Easter holidays. We will make sure that you can keep in touch with everyone by email.*

If the move is one which you are not particularly looking forward to, you should do all that you can to bring a very positive interpretation to the situation because otherwise your child will also feel uncomfortable: *There is always a lot to do when you move house and many things will be different, but together we will make sure that the new house is just as comfortable as this one is and that you make plenty of new friends at your new school. I am looking forward to starting a new job/choosing some new furniture/working in the new garden, etc. What are you looking forward to?* You can ask about what she is worrying about but be careful that you do not make promises which you alone cannot implement.

Your child should make several visits to the new house before you actually move in so that the layout becomes familiar. Bedrooms should have been allocated already, preferably after discussion, and the new positioning of her bedroom furniture should be planned carefully.

Listen carefully to what she says about school, and the people with whom she is establishing new friendships, and encourage her to invite them home. Become involved but do not overwhelm her with social commitments. She will find the newness of everything exciting but needs to decide for herself which leads she wishes to follow up.

The approach of puberty

It is preferable to spread discussions about puberty out rather than having one Big Talk. There are a great many facts to assimilate and she will find it less overwhelming if you provide the information over time.

Most children are fascinated by how their body works and when the subject crops up, and you think the child is ready to hear more, you can start talking about the process of moving towards becoming an adult and all that this involves. Always answer honestly and use terms which others beyond the family will understand. Children discuss puberty among themselves and by talking about it openly with your child you will help her to deal with some of the misinformation which may come her way and you will also be able to make everything sound normal and positive, rather than something to be afraid of and about which no one talks.

There is no exact age for the onset of puberty, but over time it has tended to begin earlier, and your child may reach it long before you did. For boys most changes happen from about 10 to 18 years. Girls can begin their periods at any time between 8 and 16 years.

There are some common principles for both boys and girls, but discussions will need to be tailored to the gender of your child. The onset of puberty can cause a child to experience strong mood swings. If the adult, as well as the child, understands that this is a normal part of growing up, it can help to prevent relationship problems in the home.

Discussions with the young child of either gender should include:

- Confirmation that she understands that her body is special and that as she grows up it will change to look more like those of the adults around her. All these changes are perfectly normal, but they happen to people at different ages.
- Reference to which parts of the body are private (refer to these as the parts under the swimwear).
- An understanding that these parts are only touched in private places like the bathroom or bedroom. At the same time it is a good idea to discuss who is allowed to touch these parts since this understanding could be useful in providing protection from sexual abuse.

Both boys and girls need to know how their bodies will change before this begins. A checklist of topics needs to include the following:

Girls

- Breasts: a gradual growth and filling out will mean that she needs to wear a bra. Enquire whether anyone else is wearing one yet. If not, this could cause embarrassment at school. Turn this into a positive by saying that all the other girls will be interested, and probably quite envious.
- Pubic and underarm hair: this is normal for girls as well as boys. Many women shave their underarm hair and some girls may worry that they are becoming male because they have not seen women with this hair.
- Body shape becomes more curvy: the hips get wider and the waist smaller, with perhaps some fat around the stomach.
- Body size: feet, hands, arms and legs sometimes grow more quickly than the trunk, which can cause some temporary clumsiness.
- Skin: sweat and oiliness develop, so good personal hygiene needs to become a habit. Remember to provide suitable aids to cleanliness. Acne can be the cause of much anxiety and should be taken seriously. There is a great deal which can be done to help to control it and the doctor will be able to offer help and guidance with this.
- Menstruation: this needs a list of headings all of its own:
  - *What is actually happening during the monthly period* – refer to the ovaries and the vagina. A picture of the female organs will help. Explain that the job of the ovaries is to produce eggs ready for when a grown woman decides to have a baby. The ovaries do this from puberty until a woman is about 50. Each month an egg gets ready to help make a baby but if it is not needed the body has to get rid of the tissues and cells. They turn into a fluid which includes blood and this comes out of the body through the opening between the legs. The period is likely to last from 3 to 7 days and the loss of blood is relatively small compared with how much we have in our bodies.
  - *Feminine protection* – explain about the range of pads and tampons and have them ready in the house. A trip to the supermarket will serve to illustrate the great range of products on the market. Suggest that the girl starts with pads but once the monthly period has become a regular feature you can offer

tampons as an alternative. Be sure that she knows how to dispose of feminine products safely and make it possible for her to do this without any embarrassment.

- *The monthly cycle* – this may not be regular for quite some time. She is not pregnant if she does not get another period next month unless she has had sexual intercourse, in which case tell her that she needs to check for a possible pregnancy.
- *Side effects* – may include: stomach cramps, bloating, soreness or swelling in the breasts, headaches and sudden mood changes such as sadness or irritability. These need not be discussed if they do not arise.
- *Sport and swimming* – these can carry on as normal if the appropriate protection is worn.

Boys

- Body size: feet, hands, arms and legs sometimes grow more quickly than the trunk, which can cause some temporary clumsiness.
- Body shape: the shoulders get broader and he gets taller. Muscles begin to develop but they should not be rushed through over-strenuous exercise or weight training.
- Voice: this gets deeper and the process may begin by 'cracking', which happens to all boys and is not something to worry about.
- Hair: this will grow on his face, arms, legs, under the arms and in the pubic area. It may also appear on the chest, but some men do not grow hair there. Make available the equipment needed for shaving the face.
- Skin: sweat and oiliness develop, so good personal hygiene needs to become a habit. Remember to provide suitable aids to cleanliness. Acne can be the cause of much anxiety and should be taken seriously. There is a great deal which can be done to help to control it and the doctor will be able to offer help and guidance with this.
- Penis: the penis and testes get bigger. He may have more erections than he has had because of the increase in sex hormones in his body. Sometimes he may find that semen is released from the penis during an erection. This can happen when he is asleep and is called a 'wet dream'. It is nothing to worry about and is perfectly normal. (If you think that the boy would like to change the bedding tell him how to do this. Do not make any reference to

additional laundry.) Explain that this semen is capable of making a girl pregnant.

Boys and girls

It is a good idea to outline for both sexes what changes the opposite sex will experience at puberty.

Besides the physical manifestations that the onset of puberty has begun, children will be experiencing emotional changes and these can cause difficulties for them and between them and their parents if they are not recognized and understood. Among the issues which can arise are:

- Caring more about what others think about their physical appearance.
- Feeling that they want to separate from their parents and spend more time with others of the same age.
- Wanting to belong to the dominant group within the social scene.
- The desire to have a boyfriend or girlfriend.

Parents should begin to allow their child to have more personal time, but remember that they are still children and will need careful guidance for many years yet, if they are to become responsible adults.

Sex

Children need to know about sex long before they reach puberty. Sex education should be seen as an ongoing responsibility, which begins when your child becomes aware of her own body. The best approach is to answer questions as they arise. Listen carefully to what your child asks, and only supply her with information she is capable of understanding at that time. If the questions come when you feel unprepared, or it is not the right time to hold the conversation, tell her that you will talk about it later. Later should not be next month. It needs to be very soon and she will be satisfied if you say exactly when you plan to return to the topic.

You need to set aside a period of time when you will not be distracted. Having a suitable reference book, with illustrations, may help you get started, especially if you are talking to a very young child. Older children may have seen explicit or suggestive images in the media or heard about sex from the lyrics of songs and such experiences could be discussed. Whatever the age of the child, any conversation about sex should include emotional considerations as well as the biological facts.

You will need to talk about:

- The fact that it is perfectly normal to be interested in sex.
- A young child will probably ask about how babies get into, and out from, their mother's tummy. Talking about a special seed which both Mummy and Daddy have, but which can't make a baby on its own, will be a good starting point. Telling her that a baby (her) started to grow inside a special part of Mummy's tummy when Daddy's seed met up with Mummy's, may well be sufficient and is a good place to stop a first conversation. If more is asked for, go on to tell her that you choose to have a baby because you love the other parent so much. Tell her that when you love someone a lot and you have decided that you want to make a baby together, you have very special cuddles so that Daddy's seed can meet up with Mummy's.
- Older children may want to know about the mechanics of conception, and you should explain it carefully and accurately using words which the child already uses to describe her anatomy, but also referring to the correct biological names. The older the child, the more important it becomes to relate sex to love and caring for oneself, as well as one's partner.
- As soon as you think she is ready, you can begin to talk about the responsibility that comes with being sexually active, since this will, when her time comes, help her to make considered decisions about how far she wishes to take things. Research indicates that calm, objective discussion, where a child feels that she can ask questions and talk about her thoughts as she needs to, can lead to her postponing initial sexual encounters beyond the early teen years.

Weddings

The child needs to be well prepared for public ceremonies, especially if she is to participate. Children may find such events overly long and not much of a spectacle. It is important that she does not distract attention from the principals, and vital that she does not spoil any recording which may be being made.

Think carefully about whether you should take your child along with you. Do not be offended if she has not been invited. Many couples are working to a budget and decide not to include children in their special day.

If the child will be attending, these are some considerations:

- Will there be other children present? This can be an advantage and a disadvantage. Other children can assist in entertaining your child, but a group needs supervision.
- Your child needs a full explanation of the format and venue of the ceremony itself, and guidelines as to how she must conduct herself while the photographs are being taken, and afterwards at the reception:
  - *John and Mary have been planning their wedding for a very long time and have only invited those people they really want to be there to share this special day with them. We are very lucky to be going. Have any of your friends been to a wedding recently?*
  - *At weddings there are always things to look at – everyone will be very interested in what people are wearing. There will be flowers and decorations in the church and at the reception. We can discuss what you thought about it all afterwards.*
  - *The venue is a very special place and everyone will be on their best behaviour – adults as well as children. I know that you will want the day to be lovely for everyone and will behave in such a way as to make me proud of you.*
  - *After the service everyone takes lots of photos. This can take a long time. If it looks as if it is going to, I will ask someone to take you for a walk until it is finished.*
  - *We will be having lunch at the reception and then there will be some speeches. These can take a long time too, but it is polite and important to sit and listen carefully. Sometimes the speeches are quite funny.*

- If the child needs to attend a rehearsal, keep telling her how well she is doing. Do not tell her that everyone will be looking at her on the day because shrinking violets will be overwhelmed and the more confident may choose to play to the gallery. It is better to reinforce the message of how special it is that she has been chosen and place emphasis on the fact that she is there to help the bride and groom. Remind her that she has to keep very still when the photos are being taken, but do not tell her to smile. Children can produce very unrealistic smiles. Aim for spontaneity.

Funerals

As adults we appreciate the fact that a funeral can help us to move forward in the grieving process. Young children are not able to understand this in the same way and their experience of a funeral will focus entirely on what is happening and the extremely emotional situation. Each family needs to decide for themselves whether or not they wish their child to attend a funeral. It is worth considering:

- How well the child knew the deceased.
- The format of the ceremony.
- How to prepare her for what is going to happen.
- How the adults are going to be able to manage their grief on the day of the funeral.
- In the case of a young child, what she will do during the service.
- Whether someone more removed from the grieving might assist in caring for the young child during the service, and at the gathering afterwards.

If the child was closely related to the deceased, and is of an age to feel the impact of the death, it is probably best that she attends the funeral, because in later life she may feel that she was excluded from saying goodbye. If the person was not very close to the child, but was to you, the case for taking her along is not so strong.

Once the decision to include her has been taken, it is essential that you explain exactly what is going to happen: *We will be going to the church for Granny's funeral the day after tomorrow. We have the funeral so that we can say our last goodbyes. There will be a lot of people there and many of them will find it quite a sad time. I know that I will. You will sit at the front of the church with me.* If the child is under 7, you can say: *I have asked . . . . . .* (a close family friend) *to come along too and she will sit with us and help me to look after you.*

Go on to explain the format: *Just before the service starts they will bring the coffin into the church. The coffin has a lid on it and I have arranged for some flowers to be placed on it and your message will be there with mine. We will sing some hymns and say some prayers and . . . . . .* (mention who) *will read something special out for us. The vicar will lead the service. It will last for about half an hour.*

If your child is under 7, say: *We will take some books for you to read during the service.* (Mention who) *. . . . . . will enjoy reading them quietly with you.*

If there is to be a cremation service, this should also be explained in the same way, leaving out the details about what happens to the coffin after the service if your child is under 7 and you think the information might upset her. If she asks, you can say: *Some time after the service we will be able to put Granny's ashes in a special place so that we always know where she was buried. We will visit it sometimes, maybe on the date of her birthday.* If she asks for even more information, you can tell her that there is a special furnace at the crematorium which is used just for looking after those who have died.

If there is to be a burial you should explain in the same way that this is Granny's special place.

Very young children should be taken away promptly after the service if there is a lot of standing around outside the church because they will not find the adult conversation interesting and will be affected by the sad atmosphere. They can be taken on to where the gathering is to be held and given some refreshments ahead of the arrival of the other mourners.

Be prepared for them to continue to ask questions about what happens to someone after they have died/are buried. This is not ghoulish, they are just seeking information. Only supply the barest of details to the very young child.

Bereavement

The way in which you manage your own grief, and that of your child, will provide her with an important experience of one of life's most significant challenges. No one will expect you to be unfailingly cheerful, so do not let unexpected setbacks convince you that you are failing to cope.

No two deaths will be the same, so there is no best-fit template of how to manage. The deceased may be a member of the immediate or extended family or could be someone well known to the child, but not in such a way as to significantly alter her life. The death might have occurred after a long illness and therefore have been expected, or it might have resulted from an accident. You may be mourning the passing of a child or an elderly person.

The first thing to consider is how much information your child can realistically absorb. Keep all conversations as factually true as you can, but avoid giving too much detail if you think it will add to her distress. An initial checklist should include the following topics, but only you will know when the time is right to address each one:

- When the person died.
- The cause of death.
- Where the person's body is at the moment.
- What happens to the person's soul after death (if you have a particular belief about this).
- The impact that this death will have on how everyone is feeling, making sure that she understands that it is perfectly acceptable to feel unhappy or cross, for instance, and that it helps to share these feelings and to talk about them with other people.
- What is going to happen over the next few days, especially if the adult(s) are going to have to go away to help attend to any arrangements for the funeral.

In some instances it may be that the death has brought an end to suffering. This can be explained to the child, but do not be surprised if it fails to ease her grief if she has lost someone very close to her. Initially she will only be able to relate to her own physical and emotional reactions.

Remember to tell the child's teacher what has happened immediately and ask that you are kept informed of how the school thinks that she is coping. They may see some behaviour which you do not and it is very helpful to get another perspective. School will provide continuity and a place removed from what may be an emotionally charged home environment and the child should return as soon as practicable.

It is possible that she finds herself mourning someone who was closer to her than they were to you, for instance, a classmate. In this situation you need to find out as much as you can about the deceased, and what happened, so that you can contribute suitably in conversation.

If your child does not seem to be able to communicate her grief she will need help to do this. Create times when you talk about the deceased and how he or she is still being missed. Ask the child what she misses most about not having the person around, but quickly move the conversation round to positives:

- What made the person laugh.
- What the person was especially good at.
- Mention experiences which were shared with the deceased.
- Mention how the deceased would have reacted in ongoing situations.

Do what you can to keep the child's memories of the person fresh.

3

Relationships

Children mature and develop at different rates, but from about the age of 6 they will begin to establish relationships with others beyond their immediate family. Parents need to maintain a watching brief in order to ensure that the relationships are mutually beneficial.

These new connections are made, and broken, as the child seeks to consolidate his feelings of self-awareness and independence. He will need to apply a range of life skills in order to build positive relationships, and you can help him develop these from an early age.

Listening

While all parents aspire to enjoy good communication with their child, many children regularly complain about the fact that their parents do not listen to them. By 'listening', the child is really asking for your undivided attention. If you are a receptive listener he will come to you to share the important things in his life. Failing to listen in this way may well result in his turning to others, who are more readily prepared to show their interest.

It will help your child to develop good listening skills if you:

- Give him your full attention when he needs or asks for it. He will realize that you are focused on the conversation if you maintain good eye contact and punctuate what he is saying with a listening response such as: *Yes, Really, Mmmm* or *I see*. Do not allow anything to distract you from listening and do not interrupt his train of thought. If what he is saying triggers an emotional reaction in you, you must do everything you can to control this. If, for instance, he perceives that you are angry, he will close down the conversation very rapidly.
- Create situations in which he is encouraged to talk. Asking him to tell you how school went is a much better conversation opener than saying: *Did you have a good day?* The latter can be answered

succinctly with a yes or no, while the former is much more open-ended. You can extend the conversation by asking follow-up questions using the child's own phrasing or vocabulary: *You said lunch was delicious. Which bit did you like best? Would you like me to cook macaroni cheese more often, as you like it so much?*

- Allow him time to organize his thoughts. We all think faster than we can speak and children are not always articulate at the first attempt. You must make him feel that he can have as much of your time as he needs, to talk about what he wants to say.

- Observe his non-verbal language. You can often learn more from *how* he says what he needs to, rather than from the actual words spoken.

- Empathize with what he is telling you. You can say: *It sounds as if wet playtime was really annoying. I hope it is dry tomorrow so that you can get out to play.* By summarizing his thoughts in your own words you are extending his vocabulary, which will mean that he will be better able to express himself in the future.

Parents do not always agree with their child. This should not prevent you from listening further, once it becomes apparent that his views are different from yours. In this situation he needs to know that you have understood what he is saying. For instance, if he tells you that he does not want to wear his sunhat because it is old-fashioned you can say: *I know that sunhats are not exactly high fashion, but I am not going to change my position, which is that you must wear one while we are out in the full sun.* He will know from your answer that you listened to his reasoning. He may not like it, but at least he is learning that you do listen.

Love

From a relatively early age children will become aware that adults talk about loving each other, their children, members of the extended family, others close to them and their pets. Children are encouraged to sign off their letters with the expression, 'with love from . . . . . .', and many of the stories they read for themselves, or have read to them, include references to love.

Parents may find it difficult to talk about what love actually means to them. Children feel more comfortable when issues are explained within a context and it may be both helpful, and easier, to talk about how being in love makes you want to behave. Examples for a very young child might be:

- *When you get hurt I want to cuddle you and make the pain go away.*
- *When there is only one chocolate biscuit left, and I want it, I let you have it because I know that you will enjoy it and that makes me feel happy.*
- *Even when I give you the last biscuit I do not expect you to give me anything back.*

As a child gets older he needs to learn that love is more abstract than merely giving something to someone who is close to you:

- *I know that your sister can be annoying, but when she gives me a hug, and tells me she loves me, I forget all about when she shouted at me.*
- *When I kiss Daddy it gives me a warm feeling inside because I know that we love each other so much.*
- *Even though we sometimes get angry with each other we both know that if either of us was in trouble the other would come running.*

He also needs to know that being in love is a wonderful feeling, but that you can only really be truly in love when you trust the other person completely. This relies on knowing a great deal about the object of your love, which takes time.

It is worth explaining that there are different degrees of love – the love a child feels for a pet will be different from that which he feels for a parent.

When adults fall out of love, the child will not, initially, be able to fully understand the reasons for this change of heart. What he needs to know is that it is not his fault. He also needs to see that the adults can still relate to each other in such a way as to make sure that the child's world is not turned completely upside down. Always ensure that the child understands what the practical implications of this change will be for him.

Loyalty

Parents should not take their child's loyalty for granted. When a child is experiencing domestic instability he may find it difficult to feel equally loyal towards both parents.

In this situation the child will absorb, and ultimately reflect, the prevailing attitude as demonstrated by either parent towards the other, unless both go out of their way to be even handed. Whichever parent is seemingly the instigator of change, the other one must do all he or she can to present the child with as neutral a perspective as possible about the situation: *We have a problem at the moment so your father has gone to live with his friend while we try to work things out. When we talk to him we can tell him about how you are getting on at school and what we did at the weekend.*

Studies of siblings of disabled people indicate that it is not unusual for a close, and very loving, bond to exist between them and their disabled sibling, but it is also true to say that the usual issues which arise between siblings can become exaggerated. For instance, the able-bodied child may feel that he is not receiving as much attention as his disabled sibling or he may realize that family outings are restricted. He may feel embarrassed about how his sibling behaves in public and it is quite possible that he is teased or even bullied because of his disabled brother or sister. Any or all of these scenarios may generate a feeling of resentment, which can test loyalty to its limits.

Parents can do a great deal to help:

- Make dedicated, special time available for both siblings separately, when they receive your undivided attention or undertake activities of their own choosing.
- Highlight the similarities common to both siblings and talk about how the able-bodied child should explain his sibling's condition to his friends. Rehearse how to deal with unpleasant remarks.
- Socialize with other families where there is a child with a similar disability.
- Organize short-term care for the disabled child for when the able-bodied one needs you to attend a school/social function in which he is involved.
- Engage in activities in which all can contribute positively.

- Take your child along to special events which celebrate the achievements of the disabled.
- Discuss the situation with the teachers so that they know the details of the disability and what effect this is having on family life.
- Make quite sure that the sibling is aware of the prognosis for his disabled sibling. He will find this easier to deal with than uncertainty.
- Remind them that able-bodied people can behave in ways which cause others to be embarrassed.

Patience

Children need to develop patience to do well at school because there they are one among many, all with needs which must be met, and also because successful relationships sometimes require us to suppress our own needs in favour of those of others. If a child is not good at managing his frustration when he has to wait his turn, he may rapidly resort to overly assertive or even aggressive behaviour.

The following guidance may be of help to parents wishing to encourage patient behaviour:

- Remember that very young children do not have an accurate concept of time. What seems like a short period to you may feel like an eternity to the four-year-old. Telling him that you will be ready in a minute and then not being available for half an hour is not helpful. Instead, tell him what you have to do before you can give him the attention he seeks: *We will set out the train set after I have cleared away the breakfast. While you are waiting you can sort out all the engines.*
- If he manages to occupy himself for the time it takes you to complete what it is you need to do first, reward the positive behaviour by telling him how pleased you are: *Thank you for being so helpful while I had to put things away. It is good to see that you can be so patient.*
- Be sure to keep your side of the bargain. If you fail to do this he will soon work out for himself that there is no point in waiting, and his exasperation will quickly erupt into negative behaviour.

- If you experience frustration because of some delay in achieving an objective, you can use this situation to reinforce how annoying it can be, but move on to show your child the best way of dealing with it: *I really get annoyed when the bus is late, but I suppose it must be because the traffic is bad. While we are waiting we can count how many red cars go past.*
- An older child should be reasoned with if you require him to wait. You can point out *why* he has to wait, and discuss any possible alternatives. In so doing you will help him to develop his ability to make well-considered choices and to respond in a mature way when he has to defer gratification: *I know you want to go bowling with me this Saturday morning, but I am afraid that I have already arranged to have my hair cut. We could go next Saturday morning instead or, if you prefer, we could go during the afternoon, after my hair appointment.*
- Avoid overcrowding your child's life with activities which take up all his potential 'down time'. Having a frenetic social life will prevent him from learning how to amuse himself, as he will be constantly looking for the next distraction.
- Arrange for some long-term goals to be shared within the family, such as redecorating his bedroom. Engage him in this right from the start by including him in choosing the colour scheme, asking him to pack his things away temporarily and even getting him to do some appropriate part of the work. He will understand that there is enormous satisfaction to be gained from taking time to do a job well. By developing a future-orientated view of life he will be better able to achieve long-term success in later life.
- If faced with behaviour which is unacceptable, and which has been triggered by a lack of patience, remain calm. Firmly explain that you can understand why he is so cross, but say that he is only making the situation worse by behaving in such a way. Do not indulge him by giving in.

Promises

Children mimic their parents and if they are in the habit of having promises made to them, they will do the same with their friends. This is fine unless they go on to break them. Parents should be very careful about making promises because children have a tremendous facility for remembering a promise and will rapidly lose trust in you if you let them down, even if there is a very good reason for doing so. Also, circumstances may change, making it impossible for you to keep the promise.

There are many reasons why children make promises. Some are made voluntarily, others as a result of coercion. Some are made flippantly, others are taken very seriously. A promise may be used:

- To get him out of a difficult situation: *I'll ring you later.* Or: *I have to go home now, but I'll bring you a bag of crisps tomorrow.*
- To get what he wants: *If you buy me the trousers I want, I'll keep my room tidy.*
- To establish a hold over someone: *I won't tell the teacher that you tore the page in the book if you will come round and play football after school.*

Discussions about making promises should include the following:

- Establishing why there is a need for a promise to be made. *Why do you want me to promise to see you after school? I usually do. The only times I can't are when I have to do my homework, or when my mum wants me to do something else.*
- Making the point that you always keep your word and so it should not require a promise: *I always do what I say I will, so why do you think I won't this time?*
- Pointing out that it will not be a good idea to promise something because things may get in the way: *I can't promise to go to the school disco because I am not sure if my mum will let me.*
- Establishing that things may need to be changed if something important intervenes: *I would really like to come round to your house for a sleepover on Friday, but my gran is ill and so Mum may have to go away to look after her. If she does, I can't come.*
- Reassuring him that not making a promise can be difficult, but that it is best if he is in any doubt about why he is being asked to commit himself, or feels that he may not be able to deliver. *I know you want me to promise, but I can't at the moment. Ask me another time.*
- Telling him that good friends don't need promises because they will trust you to do what you say you will and they will always understand if, in the event, something prevents you from doing it.

- Advising him that it is perfectly acceptable to say: *I know I made a promise, but I can't keep it because I've thought about it and I now see that it would get me into trouble.*
- Reminding him that *if* he wants to make a promise it should be one he can keep and not one dictated by someone else. He could say: *I hope that I will be able to go to the match with you, but I need to check first.*
- Finally tell him that extracting promises is not the best foundation for lasting friendships. People prefer to feel equal to their peers and if you try to make people promise things, they will think that you are taking too much control.

Sibling rivalry

Most siblings quarrel from time to time. They may compete for attention or strive to be the favoured child. The positive side of sibling rivalry is that it gives children plenty of opportunity to learn to negotiate, give and take, share, wait their turn and to stand up for their rights.

- As long as the quarrel remains verbal, and not physical, encourage children to resolve their own arguments. If they learn that you will step in to sort matters out they will continually ask you to intervene. However, very young children may eventually resort to inappropriate physical contact and this should be stopped because they do not understand the potential danger.
- If they do bring their problem to you, remind them that you prefer them to find their own common ground. If this is proving impossible, give each child a few moments to speak while the other listens. You can then state what you see to be the fundamental issue. Unless there is an obvious culprit, do not try to decide who is to blame, who started the argument or who is in the right. Any discussion along these lines may prompt them to exaggerate the situation or even to lie. Do not impose your solution. They should try to find a mutually acceptable one for themselves.
- If their argument is disturbing your space, ask them to be quieter or to move somewhere else. If this does not prompt them to settle their differences, you should ask them to go to separate rooms for a while.

- Do not allow name-calling because it hurts feelings and can lead to a diminishment of self-esteem.
- Do not allow arguments to take place in public places because they upset the peace for everyone else.
- Allow each child to have ownership of their own personal possessions, but explain that sharing is a good thing to do because the time may well come when one of them wants to borrow something which does not belong to him. Taking turns with shared items in the home will help him to make, and keep, his friends at school.
- Allow each child to have his or her own personal space. Younger children should be distracted by you when the older sibling has friends home from school and the younger child should not interrupt the older child's study time.
- Never compare your children. Show them that you value them as unique, and very special, individuals. It is inevitable that, on occasion, your children will tell you that they do not think you are being fair. Do not become overly concerned by this. Things tend to balance out over time.
- Remember to reinforce their cooperative behaviour by praising them when they help each other or settle their differences for themselves.

Peer pressure

Peer pressure is a potent influence in schools, even for the young child. It is unrealistic to deny its presence. It pervades many childish discussions with the intention of getting someone to act, behave, think or look in a certain way. Once your child has moved into the world of school, with its many new and complex demands, you should constantly remind him that:

- To you he is the best thing in the world.
- It will make him feel better if he talks about any unwanted pressure which he is receiving from his peers.
- Doing what his friends want him to may seem to be the easier option at the time, but it could lead to his doing something which he will later regret.

- True friends will respect him for doing what *he* wants rather than what *they* want.
- Those who bring sustained, unwanted pressure to bear are bullies.
- Bullies need to make others do things, or undergo difficult and unpleasant experiences, so that they can feel better about themselves. They are often afraid of criticism, so they criticize first. Tell your child that he does not have to be their scapegoat.

By recognizing that peer pressure does exist, and not belittling your child's response to it, you have taken the first step towards helping him. You need to know what kind of pressure he is experiencing and he will only keep you informed if you make it comfortable for him to speak to you. If you equip your child with a few chosen responses, it will help him both to understand that he can count on your support and also respond suitably when the need arises. These responses should be rational and plausible because he may have to defend his position.

For example, you could point out that it is useful that everyone is good at different things: *It is a good thing that some people are especially good at maths because when they grow up they will be able to do the jobs which need maths, like designing bridges. Other people will do different, but very useful jobs, which they are good at.*

Or, you could explain that people need different amounts of sleep: *It is not important what time you go to bed. What is important is that you get enough sleep to be able to do all the things you want to do every day. Different people need different amounts of sleep. Perhaps I need more than you do.*

On the subject of television and the use of the computer you could suggest that your child says: *Instead of watching lots of television or playing on the computer I prefer to . . .* (mention something unusual or exciting).

Boasting

Boasting is when we elaborate on the truth or when we draw inappropriate attention to our achievements, skills or attributes. Your child may feel it necessary to boast because:

- He may be feeling inadequate or suffering from low self-esteem and be seeking to place himself in a favourable light compared to his siblings or peers.
- He may be needing some positive feedback.
- He may enjoy fooling the adults.

If you suspect that what you are being told is not the true picture, take steps to confirm your suspicions before confronting your child. You could check with the teacher or the parents of his friends, depending on the context of the boast. Once you have established that the statements are an elaboration of the true facts, ask your child to confirm what he is saying to his peers: *I have heard that you are telling your friends that our new house has an enormous garden. Why are you saying this?* How your child responds to this question will reveal whether or not he realizes that what he is saying is innocent wishful thinking or a deliberate embellishment of the facts.

Either way, children need to understand that their conversations must be based on the truth. You should explain that his friends will find out in the end if what he is saying is true or false. If true, then nothing more will be made of it. If false, there will need to be some complicated re-establishment of the truth, which can be very embarrassing and lead to a loss of trust among friends.

You should give some thought as to why a child indulges in boasting and use this situation as an opportunity to discuss the positives in the child's life and to celebrate his achievements and skills.

Bullying

Bullying is repeated harassment, over a period of time, carried out in such a way that it makes it difficult for the victim to defend himself. Without adult intervention at an early stage, bullying can lead to emotional, social and academic problems.

There are three main types of bullying:

1 Verbal, which includes:
   - Teasing
   - Sarcasm

- Name-calling
- Discriminatory remarks based, for example, on ethnicity, social background, intellectual capacity or gender

2 Physical, which includes:
- Pushing, hitting, kicking and punching
- Any unwanted physical contact
- Taking someone else's possessions

3 Indirect bullying, which includes:
- Spreading rumours or starting gossip about someone
- Excluding someone
- Getting someone into undeserved trouble
- Sending hurtful text or email messages

Parents should not wait until they suspect that their child is being bullied before addressing this within the family. However, creating an expectation that bullying is endemic and that your child will experience it at some time or other is not recommended because it will over-sensitize him. Instead, parents should make it clear from an early age that they would like to share their child's negative as well as positive experiences. This way he will feel able to talk about the highs and lows of school life and parents will be able to detect any emerging pattern which needs their intervention.

Very young children are not expert at masking their emotions and you may observe that your child's behaviour has changed.

- He may have become depressed or withdrawn.
- He may start making transparent, and regular, excuses as to why he should not go to school.
- He may seem perfectly happy at home, but the teacher tells you that things are not going smoothly at school.
- You may even see bruises or other physical injuries which are not explained plausibly.

Once you have established that your child is being bullied, you should tell him that:

- It is the person doing the bullying who is doing something wrong, and that, as the victim, he is not the guilty party.
- He is not alone in being the victim of bullying. Surveys indicate that as many as half of all children are bullied at some time

during their school years and at least 10 per cent are bullied on a regular basis.

- Bullies tend to target children who are loners, appear passive or who do not fit the dominant group's exacting, and often totally unrealistic, set of standards concerning physical or mental attributes.
- Bullies may have been the victims of bullying in the past. They are certainly unhappy people who are seeking to take their frustrations out on innocent people.
- Bullying only thrives because people do not feel able to stand up to it.
- The best way of dealing with it is to ignore it, because if you do not give the perpetrator the satisfaction of responding to it, he will quickly realize that there is little point in bullying you.
- By walking away purposefully you show the bully that you are no easy target.
- Your child is less likely to be bullied if he stays in the company of other children.

You must make the school aware of what is going on. All schools have a duty to take bullying seriously and they will want to hear of it as soon as possible so that they can take immediate steps to eradicate it.

Ask the school:

- What they are going to do about it.
- How they will keep you informed as to any actions they have taken.

Tell them how you intend to provide them with feedback as to your child's ongoing state of mind, but avoid doing this in front of him.

Keep the channels of communication open with your child and between home and school so that any recurrence can be dealt with at a very early stage.

In these days of information and communication technology new forms of bullying are becoming commonplace. Bullying online or via a mobile phone has become a recognized way of exerting undesirable pressure on another person. Tell your child that he should only give out his contact details to close friends. Regularly remind him that, as part of the agreement relating to his having access to a phone or the internet, you need him to tell you if he is receiving unsolicited messages. In such circumstances you can do several things:

- Tell him never to retaliate with similarly unpleasant messages, but instead he should show them to you.
- Keep a record of the sender's number or email address and the time and date of the contacts.
- Tell the police about it because the perpetrator could be breaking the law.
- Try to get the service provider to block messages from the sender.
- Change your child's phone number or email address.

You may become aware that your child is the one doing the bullying. If so, remember that it is often a cry for help or a desire for attention. Keep calm, but take steps to establish why he feels the need to behave in this way. Tell him that you do not condone his behaviour in any way, but assure him that you are there to help him resolve any problems. Discuss:

- Why he has chosen the victim as a target.
- What he has actually done and how long it has been going on.
- How he proposes to put it right.

Make sure that he knows that you are in regular contact with the school and are supporting them in making sure that there will never be a recurrence.

Gossip

Like many adults, children engage in gossip. If parents discover that their child is either the perpetrator or the victim of gossip, they should do all they can to eradicate what can be very damaging behaviour as soon as it is detected. At its worst, gossip causes a child's self-esteem to plummet and it will certainly have an impact, which may be long term, on friendships and relationships. Furthermore, research shows that gossiping can become a habit. This is another justification for early intervention.

First, you will need to explain the difference between talking and gossiping to your child. The main points to get across are that *gossip* is:

- A way of speaking about someone else which may make that person feel unhappy or angry.
- When someone deliberately says something which is not true about someone else.
- When someone tells someone else something about another person which was supposed to remain private.

By comparison, *talking* is how you share your thoughts, ideas and experiences with the people around you. Children need to understand that they may talk about someone else, but it should always be in a factual and positive way and reflect their loyalty towards the other person. It is perfectly acceptable to say: *James is really good at playing football. I wish I could score goals like him.* Or: *Ellie tells really good jokes. She makes me laugh.*

It will help if you tell your child why people feel the need to spread gossip, i.e.:

- They may wish to boost their own social status within the group.
- They may be seeking attention from their peers.
- They may think it is funny.
- They may use it as a way of gaining revenge.

So, how should your child deal with gossip if he finds himself hearing it? Tell him:

- That other children will eventually think well of him if he tells them that he will not listen to gossip.
- That he should never pass on unkind things which he may hear about someone.
- That he should tell the teacher if he believes that what he hears will cause the target to feel uncomfortable.

He must also understand that if someone tells him something which they consider to be private, unless he feels that it is an 'unsafe' secret, he should not tell anyone else. An unsafe secret would be anything which might place the person concerned in danger.

Were he to find himself the subject of gossip he should:

- Tell an adult how he feels about the situation. Older children may feel able to tell the perpetrator direct, but not all children will have this degree of self-confidence.
- Ignore the gossip, safe in the knowledge that the instigator has problems of his or her own, which they are not able to resolve.
- Ask trusted friends to put out messages which are based on the truth and which directly contradict the gossip.

If you find out that your child is the instigator of gossip you should discuss with him how he would feel if he was the intended victim. Ascertain *why* he feels that he needs to behave in this way and address any perceived vulnerability. You must show him that you consider gossiping to be totally unacceptable and tell him that you will support the school in making sure that it stops immediately.

Saying sorry

Like 'please' and 'thank you', sorry should be a word with which even the youngest child is familiar. He should hear adults using and meaning it as part of his daily life because, even with the best will in the world, situations regularly arise which need to be resolved with an apology.

Your child will have arguments with his friends, as well as his family, and he will commit misdemeanours, or omit to do something he should, both at home and elsewhere. He needs to learn that saying sorry will make a difference to how other people see him. He also needs to learn that any apology must be heartfelt and that his subsequent behaviour should be modified appropriately.

If he finds himself at odds with others' expectations of him, or in a situation where he has fallen out with a friend, he needs to follow these steps:

- He should take some time out to cool off.
- He should think about what has happened.
- He should make contact with the other party. If there has been an argument he should ask the other person to talk about how he or she feels and listen carefully to what they say. He should explain

how *he* feels. He should recognize that the two parties do not necessarily have to agree.

- He should understand that it is sometimes very hard to make a genuine apology, but if he is in the wrong it needs to be made so that the difficulty can be put behind him.

4

Feelings and emotions

A child knows what it feels like to be happy, sad or angry, but may not yet be able accurately to read the emotional signals given out by an adult or another child and may, for example, confuse guilt with anger.

Studies show that those children whose parents regularly discuss feelings and emotions with them are more successful in forming healthy and robust relationships in later life, and are better equipped to deal with challenging situations.

A checklist for supporting your child will include:

- Being ready to share her emotions. If she feels sad about the death of her pet, you need to show her that it is affecting you too.
- Being patient. Take time to listen.
- Not dismissing her feelings. She is feeling them acutely.
- Helping her to find solutions to what is causing her negative feelings.
- Sharing your own feelings with her and telling her how you intend to move on from feeling low, angry or out of control.

Moods

Everybody experiences different moods and they can change rapidly. One minute we might be feeling on top of the world and then something happens which instantly prompts a change of mood. It is much the same for children, with the added complication that they do not have well-developed strategies for dealing with their mood swings.

Once a child is in a bad mood, it can be difficult for her to shake it off. The effects can multiply because not only will she need to deal with the initial problem, but by behaving badly she may well cut herself off from her friends and family, who are the very people who could best help her. A good basis for a discussion with a pre-teen who is experiencing mood swings will include:

- Reassuring her that you understand how she is feeling as a result of needing to take more personal responsibility for her actions.
- Confiding in her about how you remember feeling when you were her age. You could tell her that you used to feel mixed emotions about leaving childhood behind, while at the same time looking forward to being a teenager.
- Boosting her self-esteem because she is becoming more self-critical and analytical as a result of drawing personal comparisons with her peers.
- A reminder that it is not always her fault that she feels as she does; it could be because of the biological changes which are occurring within her.
- Some practical strategies for dealing with her moods. She could write a private diary in which her thoughts and feelings can be freely expressed, take some exercise, get enough sleep and allow herself to cry.

Happiness

If asked what makes them feel happy, very young children will mention concrete things like presents, their birthday or going swimming. We need to show them that other, less tangible, things can be the source of happiness: a hug, a sunny day, a long-awaited telephone call or just relaxing with a friend, so that they learn that genuine happiness is more about feelings than possessions.

You will help her to experience true happiness if you suggest strategies such as:

- Being a kind, friendly and helpful person.
- Spending time with the family doing shared things like eating a meal together.
- Listening to music.
- Joining in with what is going on rather than merely being an observer.
- Developing a wide range of extra-curricular interests.

- Sharing what makes her happy with others and making a mental note of particularly happy times so that she can recall them when things are going less well.
- Keeping fit and well by taking exercise and eating healthily.
- Having a ready smile on her face.
- Remembering that happiness is infectious.

Unhappiness

Childhood sadness is generally transient. Unhappiness, however, can take over a child's life. The most obvious signs will be tears and she may be more clingy than usual. Changes in eating and sleeping patterns and also bowel movements may also be evident, together with tantrums, because she may feel frustrated that the cause of her misery is not being dealt with effectively either by her or those closest to her.

The first step towards helping your child is to consider any pressures which she might be experiencing. Do this before talking to her.

Once you have identified some possible causes, find a special time when it will be just you and your child together, uninterrupted, for as long as you need. It is not necessary to adopt a 'meeting' format; indeed, it is preferable if you are doing something like going for a walk with the dog or cooking. Avoid telling her to cheer up, or saying that there is nothing to be unhappy about, because it will just make the situation worse. You need to accept that she feels unhappy. Ask her how she sees the situation, because her perspective will be different from yours. Tell her that sharing feelings brings people closer together. Comments like this are helpful: *I always feel really happy when we walk the dog together* (or whatever activity it is you are doing). *When do you feel happy?*

The response to this will tell you a lot about how she is feeling. You may get an answer which gets straight to the point: *I don't feel happy now or ever any more*, or you may get a response which directly answers your question: *I feel happy when I am swimming*. Always develop the theme of happiness if it is presented to you: *Yes, we must go swimming again soon.*

If, however, you get straight into the territory of unhappiness, develop the theme by saying: *I am sorry to hear that you are feeling so unhappy. Let's talk about what is making you feel like this, because whatever it is I want to help you feel better.*

She may respond immediately and identify the causes of her unhappiness or she may refuse, or not be able to explain her emotions. If she tells you, be wary of saying that you can solve the problem. You may not be able to remove it altogether, but you must indicate that the problem is now already better for her because together you will address it: *I'll talk to Mrs Bloggs and tell her that you are finding your maths tricky and we will sort out what it is which is causing the problem.*

Or: *If Mary won't play with you at the moment we need to ask someone else home to play after school. Who would you like?*

Or: *I know that you are sad that Daddy doesn't live with us any more, but he still loves you very much and wants to know all about what you are doing.*

If you don't get to the heart of the matter from her response, you will have to make some informed guesses: *Is everything going well at school? What do you enjoy most at school? Who are your friends at the moment?*

Or: *Did you enjoy going to Daddy's new house at the weekend?*

Or: *What does it feel like being a big sister/brother?*

When you take time to talk about her unhappiness with your child, she will learn that it is acceptable to share her feelings, that you will take them seriously, and that she can count on your support. She will gradually learn that unhappiness is a fact of life for everyone and that sometimes we all have to accept that things cannot change. Do not make the mistake of thinking that her unhappiness will go away if you wait long enough. She needs help to deal with it now.

Sharing what makes you unhappy with her will help her to realize that we all feel like this from time to time. Finally, reassure her that it is perfectly acceptable to let the feeling of unhappiness go after a significant event such as bereavement.

Excitement

A child feels this emotion very strongly. In the lead up to a particularly exciting event it will help if you:

- Keep your child's routine stable. Bedtimes, meals and other routine events should carry on as normal because they provide stability and security.
- Avoid giving her extra snacks which are likely to give her a sugar rush. Sweet foods provide a short-lived burst of energy but she will experience fatigue as the effect wears off. These highs and lows can exacerbate difficult behaviour.
- Keep her safety in mind. Make sure she does not put herself in danger.

Jealousy

Young children can find it very hard to share, and this applies to people as well as to material possessions. This can sometimes cause them to feel acutely jealous or to vehemently declare that the world is not a fair place. Children will also desire things which are not theirs. Jealousy can be very difficult to dissipate without your help and understanding.

The checklist for dealing with jealousy, or the strongly held feeling that things are not fair, should include:

- Not giving in to what the child wants. You can explain that you understand what she feels like when she sees that her friend has exactly the pair of shoes she would like, but tell her that she cannot have them *because* . . .
- Recognizing that her feelings are strong, but pointing out what *she* has, which others may be envious of.
- Congratulating her on being able to identify what it is which is making her feel jealous, but explaining that she is making things uncomfortable not only for herself but also for everyone else.
- Drawing up a list of things which you both agree are not fair. This might include calling people names, not having enough food to eat or a good home to live in. This should serve to highlight the trivial nature of her jealousy.
- Providing her with an exit strategy by helping her to apologize for her inappropriate behaviour. Tell her that you will now forget about it as long as she does not allow it to recur in the near future.

Anger

It may come as something of a shock to see your child mimicking your own, or someone else's, angry behaviour. Temper tantrums are an obvious sign of anger, but some children express this emotion less overtly and some may even suppress their feelings completely because they have come to believe that their anger prompts you to be angry with them.

Younger children

When dealing with a young child's temper tantrums it is very important that you do not respond in anger. This will merely perpetuate the situation. Hard as it may be, you are much better able to control your anger and must lead by example. Saying: *My goodness, you are feeling very cross at the moment. I feel cross too sometimes. It always helps to talk about why you are angry, but I can see that you are too cross to talk now. We can do this later, but for now why don't we . . .* (mention something that she enjoys doing)?

Later, and it may be much later, but should be the same day, you can return to the situation. Make quite sure that you have her full attention, and that you will not be interrupted, and also ensure that things are going well between you. Say: *You were very angry this morning, weren't you? I am so glad that you aren't angry now. What made you feel so cross?*

She will probably tell you, but if she can't remember, or is reluctant to refer to the incident, you need not dwell on it but should address her angry behaviour. The reason for this is that you are going to help her to develop an anger management strategy.

Anger management strategy

Start by talking about how she behaved: *When you were angry you shouted a lot and threw your toys down the stairs. Did this make you feel good?*

She will almost certainly feel embarrassed and may not be able to respond. Do not force an answer: *Instead of shouting . . . what should you have done instead?*

Some prompting may well be needed here: *I know that Mark* (sibling) *made you cross when he spoilt your model, but all you need to do is to ask me to move him when you want to build something.*

Or: *Instead of throwing your toys when you feel cross, next time say, Mummy, I feel really cross because I can't do this puzzle. Will you help me?*

Or: *When I won't let you have a chocolate bar at the shops remember that I may let you have a nice treat after tea, especially if you don't get cross.*

Remember to comment positively about good behaviour as it is happening and be especially delighted when you see her controlling herself in potentially anger-inducing situations. It is much more effective to give immediate praise than to offer it retrospectively.

And do remember that there is nothing as frustrating as being angry and not having an appreciative audience. Ignore (if at all possible) angry behaviour which is not dangerous to the child or others. The storm will pass much more quickly if you do.

Older children

The simmering anger of an older child needs a different strategy. Some children may not feel able to release their feelings and they need help to do this: *You are very quiet this afternoon. I sometimes feel quiet when I get cross. Are you feeling cross at the moment?*

The child may be relieved that you are presenting her with an opportunity to discuss how she is feeling and it will reassure her to know that you sometimes feel the same as she does. She may, or may not, be able to articulate her feelings, but again you should gently prompt her to talk them through. Reassure her that everyone feels angry from time to time. Tell her that you want to help her when she feels cross, but that you need her to tell you when, and why, she is feeling like this.

Anger management strategy

An anger management strategy for the older child should include:

- Taking time out to cool off. This will help her to stop the argument or prevent her from going on to do something which will only make matters worse.
- Identifying what caused her to feel so angry. Anger is generally triggered by some action or omission.
- Writing her thoughts down. This can be very useful, since it should

have the effect of preventing her feelings from c

- Asking herself whether this will matter in, sa'
  This should help her get matters into perspe
- Avoiding the things which cause her to be angry.
- Apologizing to those she has upset.
- Reminding her how she feels when someone is angry with

If you fail to contain your own anger, make sure that she understands why you were cross, admit that you were at fault, but suggest what could have avoided your angry response in the first place, especially if it is related to your child.

Finally it is worth remembering that, just occasionally, good things result from anger – it can prompt us to stand up for our rights or take steps to correct an injustice.

Arrogance

As children get older, they make comparisons between themselves and their peers. Parents should step in when their child flaunts what she considers to be superior attributes. These may be:

- Intellectual ability
- A specific talent
- Social status
- Material possessions

The way to deal with her own perceived intellectual or talent superiority is to confirm that she is certainly very good at whatever it is, but to go on to say that others are not so fortunate and they have to work that bit harder at the particular attribute. Then identify something which she has found more of a challenge, such as learning to swim. Remind her how she felt when she was struggling with that situation and how helpful her swimming teacher was in breaking down swimming into easier steps.

Unfavourable comparisons concerning social status or material possessions should not be condoned. You could point out that she is very lucky to live in a comfortable house, which she is only able to enjoy because of the hard work which her parents have put in over the years. Tell her that she will quickly lose friends if she continues to think of herself as being better than anyone else.

Competitiveness

..ept within acceptable boundaries, competitiveness can be a great motivator. If, however, it begins to take over life, it should be dissipated. When sports day is approaching you can encourage your child to practise for her events, but keep reminding her that it is all about taking part, doing her best and working for her team. Reassure her that you will not mind if she does not win her race. In class, she needs to learn that the teacher is not really very interested in who finishes their work first. Instead, she will expect everyone to work to the best of their ability and she will not accept a shoddy, speedily executed piece of work from someone who merely wanted to finish before everyone else.

If you are inclined to get very involved when watching your sports team, make sure that you comment favourably about the game, whatever the outcome: *I thought they played quite well, especially during the first half, but the other team out-classed them in the later stages of the match and so they deserved to win.*

The best approach is to encourage her to be competitive against herself rather than others. If she gets all her spellings right this week, then she should aim to do the same next time.

Loneliness

If a child is being rejected or victimized by her peer group, is suffering from low self-esteem, or is developmentally immature compared to her peer group, she may find herself having to deal with feelings associated with genuine loneliness.

All the adults with whom she comes into regular contact should be involved in helping her to overcome these feelings. Try to identify the causes of the problem, and discuss the results with the school. Is it possible that:

- She is behaving aggressively towards others?
- She lacks the skills or confidence to enter existing play situations?
- She is not willing to adapt her own thoughts or ideas to meet those predominating within the game?

Once the causes have been identified, you should talk with her about how she can modify her behaviour or become the kind of person people want to include in their games, or be friends with. It is important that she thinks about how others see her.

Finally, remember that being alone and feeling lonely are not the same things. Sometimes children prefer to be alone. You should only get involved if your child, or the school, mentions that she is feeling lonely.

Self-esteem

We all thrive on praise and positive feedback and children need to receive regular appreciation. Words of encouragement should feature frequently in family dialogue, with adults rewarding children as well as each other in this way, so that the children will begin to incorporate similar phrases in their own conversations.

Nurturing self-esteem should be a high priority, since children who feel good about themselves are more able to take responsibility, act independently, and take pride in what they have achieved. They are also better able to take the initiative, tolerate frustration, and help others. They respond better to peer pressure and deal with their emotions more successfully.

Poor self-esteem can develop as a result of problems at school; words said or unsaid; and actions taken or omitted – all of which have a lasting negative effect on the child. So, from an early age, you must do all you can to help her feel better about herself:

- Look for circumstances in which you can offer praise. Do not merely wait for them to present themselves.
- Teach her to make positive self-statements such as: *I was really helpful at school today. Megan fell over and I got the teacher for her.*
- Stop short of shaming her when you need to discipline her.
- Allow her to take decisions and make choices on her own and commend particularly mature or sensible ones.
- Show her that you get things wrong too but you always try to keep a sense of proportion.

Sometimes poor self-esteem can cause a child to appear shy. Different children feel shy in different situations and such feelings may be brought about as a result of nervousness, worry, fear or embarrassment. A parent will be able to recognize shy behaviour.

Your child may hang back in new situations or even go out of her way to avoid them. She will find it difficult to make eye contact and her speech may be mumbled. She may blush easily.

The best way to help her is to:

- Ask her when she feels shy. Discuss strategies which will help her. If she feels shy at someone's house, stay with her until she is clearly more comfortable. If she finds that the feelings come on at her swimming class, consider withdrawing her for a term.
- Tell her that she should not worry about her feelings of shyness because they can be quite helpful to her. For instance, they will allow her to stand back and take stock of a situation before rushing in, which may result in a better outcome for her.
- Discuss the situation with her teacher, but do not tell your child that you have done so. Ask the school to do what they can to help.
- Tell her that everyone can experience feelings of shyness, even those who appear very confident. In fact, they are sometimes hiding their shyness behind their extrovert behaviour.
- Make a list of all the things she is good at and subtly manufacture situations where she can utilize these skills in front of others.
- Tell her that there are things about herself which she cannot change, but which she should accept because they are part of her personality.

5

Anxieties

Childhood anxiety is very real. You should help your child to manage his stress and encourage him to share his problems with you. He will need to believe that you will be non-judgemental and that you will keep the information confidential until you and he have agreed otherwise. Also, teach him to recognize what it is which makes him feel anxious and how he can take steps to anticipate the problem areas. If he worries about tests at school, he could ask for help with his revision. Do tell him that we all experience stress from time to time and say that it is perfectly normal to worry. It will reassure him if you tell him that feeling nervous can actually help us to perform better.

Give him practical suggestions as to how he can manage the symptoms of stress. These might be to find something to play with, watch a DVD, listen to music or do something physical. Tell him that it is better to take these steps quickly in order to prevent the anxiety becoming established. Tell him that worries can seem huge, but it is best to try to deal with small parts of the bigger picture, one at a time.

If you do not feel that you are making progress in working through the anxiety together it may be time to ask for the support of a professional such as the health visitor, doctor or teacher.

Friendships

Children's friendships can be very volatile. One day they may be the best of friends, and the next they are at loggerheads. Your response should be to listen and make a few interested-sounding responses to the end of the day's feedback: *Oh dear! That sounds a bit tricky, how did you sort it out?* is better than: *I can't have that. I will speak to his mother tomorrow.* Tomorrow is another day and things may well settle down again. Your swift intervention could make things worse.

If, however, you begin to feel that the problems are more than a passing phase, it is time to make further enquiries. You need to find out how your child sees the problem, because it could be very different from the way you perceive it. There are any number of possible causes for friendship difficulties:

- He may find it difficult to keep friends because he is too exclusive.
- He may be trying to intrude on an already close friendship between two other children.
- He may not have much in common with the other child, but is desperate to be his or her friend because he or she is seen as the peer group leader.
- He may not be very skilled in making up after a row.
- He may be using unkind words which cause upset among the peer group.

Once you have established possible causes, you need to work out a course of action to help your child build secure friendships. Initially, suggest that he is friendly with everyone until someone emerges from the group as having well-matched interests. Talk to him about what makes a good friend. It is someone:

- he likes being with and who makes him happy
- who sticks up for him when times are difficult
- who puts up with his bad moods
- he can trust to be discreet
- who does not engage in gossip or malicious tittle-tattle
- who allows him to have time out.

A quiet word with the teacher will alert her to any problems and you will need to be prepared to hear that your child is no angel.

Solving friendship disputes takes time, but do not press him for regular updates. You will be able to tell how things are going, and whether he still needs your help.

Performance at school

When children start school, they quickly realize that they are one among several and may begin to compare themselves unfavourably to other children. A child may suddenly make the kind of comment which can worry parents: *I'm no good at maths*, or he may appear reluctant to go to school.

The first thing is to establish what has caused this. Ask yourself why he has raised the matter now. Has he experienced sudden insight, or has he been thinking about it for some time? The way to do this is to ask about school. Talk to him about the things he can do really well. If you are not clear what these may be (and be sure that there will be some aspects at which he shines – there is genius in all of us) check with the teacher. Start with comments like: *I know, because Mrs Bloggs has told me, that you are really good at . . .* Continue with: *So what else are you good at?* If you have chosen the right time to hold this conversation, he will be able to make a few suggestions. Take some time to elaborate on these successes.

If his self-esteem is very low you may get: *I am not any good at anything.* This needs to be countered immediately with: *That is not true. You are very good at . . .* (mentioning things that are applicable to the home situation). *Not everyone knows how to . . .*

You can develop the success ethic by broadening the conversation to include whatever it was which first triggered the conversation: *So, we know that you are very good at . . . but* at the moment *you are finding it difficult to . . . I know that we can do something about this together so that you will feel better about . . . very soon.*

Now you need to make an action plan together, and your child can help with this. Ask: *What do you think will help?* His answer will usually include the teacher and/or any child with whom he is comparing himself, or who has caused the problem by making an insensitive remark. Do not draw up an action plan which you will not, or cannot, implement. So do not promise to get a particular child to stop making unhelpful comments. That is beyond your power.

You can, however:

- Promise to talk to the teacher.
- Help him with whatever aspect of his school work it is that is causing the problem at home.

Unless the parent of any other child involved is a particularly understanding friend of yours, it is not a good idea to challenge him or her about their child's behaviour towards yours. Leave that to the teacher to resolve. She will be able to manage it on your behalf by talking to the other child(ren) concerned.

After a while you need to check how things are going – but not every day. After a few days, have a quiet talk with the teacher to get an update. Do not keep asking your child how it is going or keep asking the teacher in front of him. Start conversations about school with a neutral topic such as: *Did you have PE today?* Or: *What did Mr Jones talk about in Assembly?*

You should be able to tell if things are improving. If they are not, and the child keeps referring back to the issue, you need to follow the matter up with another meeting with the teacher. At this meeting ask:

- *What is the school doing to promote your child's confidence?*
- *Are all the staff aware that he needs a boost?*
- *What more can I do?*

It is always most effective if you and the school are working together. Listen hard to what they tell you, and it is just possible that they might tell you that your child could be using this matter to seek your attention or demand more of your time! Do not take this as personal criticism. It is helpful feedback.

Fear of the dark

As children get older, they will see television images and hear other children talking about frightening things, and find references to real and imagined nocturnal happenings in their books.

Bedtime avoidance tactics will be the most obvious sign that your child is afraid of the dark, but he may also seek company when going upstairs when it is dark outside, or ask for the light to be left on all night in his bedroom or on the landing. In extreme cases he will not be able to sleep alone.

Parents should recognize that this is a very real fear. Your child will feel powerless over his anxiety, and the only way he can control it is to ask for the light to be left on or for someone to accompany him upstairs. You should agree without hesitation. Furthermore, you should leave the light on all night just in case he wakes up. He needs to trust that you will stand by your actions. At this stage you should only ask more about why he wants the light on if you think there is a specific reason as to why he is making the request. Leave the matter for now if you think it is a reflection of a general fear.

Comments like this are helpful: *I am glad you asked for the light to be on because it will help us all to see well if we wake up in the night.*

After a week or so you can reopen the discussion by asking: *Do you still want the light on at night?*

Depending on his response, you can extend the conversation further with a discussion about people who work at night – policemen, firemen, nurses, doctors, the people who stack the supermarket shelves for us, etc., etc. so that he realizes that there are plenty of good people up and about during the hours of darkness. Talk about nocturnal animals – for example owls, badgers, foxes – and read stories about the people and the animals.

If you find that he is beginning to mention his concerns, these should be dealt with seriously, one by one. Comments like this are helpful: *Yes, we do have burglars, but we also have the police to look after us.* Or: *No, we do not have monsters but we do have children who enjoy trying to make other people frightened and you can now tell them that we have talked about the monsters and you know that they do not exist.* Or even: *Do you know why it gets dark? Well, I'll tell you . . .* (A short explanation of the earth's rotation could suffice, but again you may well find yourself delving into things more deeply.) Explain the benefits of darkness, stressing how we all need to sleep.

Make sure you include the comment: *We will keep the light on every night for as long as you need it. You can tell me when you don't want it any more.*

Never make fun of this fear. You must represent the voice of reason if the child is to overcome it.

Blood

Many young children are afraid of blood, and some older children find the sight of it quite traumatic. The best approach is to explain what blood does and how important it is in promoting healthy bodies. You can tell him that blood:

- Helps us to fight infections.
- Carries heat around our bodies.

- Carries oxygen and other vital chemicals around our bodies to where we need them and also takes waste materials to the parts of the body responsible for eliminating them.
- Allows all the energy which food gives us to move around our bodies.

Some children worry that if they cut themselves they will bleed to death. You can reassure your child on this point by telling him that blood is able to make a sort of web over a cut, which allows a clot to form so that the blood stops flowing.

Crime and burglary

Children see and hear a great deal about crime from the media. They may worry about being the victim of a crime. They may also worry about people they are close to getting involved in crime.

If a child has been directly affected by a crime he will feel similar emotions to those of the affected adults, but very young children will not be able to articulate their concerns. Instead, parents may see physical manifestations of their child's anxiety: fear of the dark, resisting separation from their parents, a poor sleeping pattern and complaints about feeling unwell would be typical. During the immediate aftermath of the incident he will be absorbing the reaction of the adults, which will cause him additional stress.

Children need explanations, so you should give him as much information as you can, based on the evidence as you know it: *The burglar had no job and he takes drugs. He needed money to get his drugs and so he broke into our house to take things which he could sell, to get money. The police have given us some advice as to how we can make sure that this does not happen again and we will be putting more locks on the doors and windows.*

Do not be surprised if your child keeps returning to the incident in his conversations. This is his way of coming to terms with what has happened. Equally, do not be surprised if he does not wish to talk about it. If this is the case it might be helpful to ask him what he thinks you should do to make him feel safer. His answer will let you know how far he has travelled along the road to recovery. If he tells you that he does not know, you should interpret this as his not yet having come to terms with the incident and you should keep on creating subtle opportunities for him to talk about it. If he comes up with a practical, well thought out suggestion, you will know that he is beginning to move on.

If the incident affected him directly, you need to reassure him that you do not mind that, for instance, his mobile phone was stolen, because he is safe and that is all that matters. Furthermore, you should let him know that you do not attach any blame to him for what happened.

Pain

A surgical procedure or significant illness may cause a child to experience pain. If treatment is planned ahead of time there are several things you can do to help him prepare for it:

- Tell him that you will be there throughout, even when he is asleep.
- Tell him, in simple terms, what is going to happen. Include references to needles and why they will be part of the treatment programme. Use puppets or dolls to explain things to a very young child.
- Tell him that you, and the doctors, are there to help him feel better and so he should tell you how he is feeling so that you can do something about it.
- Tell him, if it is true, that he will be able to choose whether he sits up or lies down in bed for his treatment. This will make him feel that he can influence what is happening.

In the immediate post-operative phase you can help him through the pain by teaching him how to breathe deeply. You should have a multitude of activities lined up which will serve to distract him during moments of crisis and continually give physical comfort by hugging and touching him.

6

Health and safety

Parents have a responsibility to ensure that their child's world is safe from danger. Children need to understand why they are being shielded from some risk-associated situations and also that there are agencies on hand to help when outside intervention is needed.

Medical specialists

Visits to hospital, the doctor, dentist, etc. should be seen as a normal part of life. Any concerns you may have should be kept under wraps, since they are likely to make your child anxious about the situation. Remember that the happier and more relaxed she is, the quicker she will get over her treatment.

Doctor

It is essential to explain why a visit to the doctor is needed. In order to make a visit to the surgery as positive an experience as possible you should:

- Take your young child with you when you, or her sibling, needs to see the doctor because it will help her to learn about visiting the surgery. If, on the other hand, you anticipate that treatment likely to upset her will be administered, it would be better if you arrange childcare.
- Understand that she may exhibit atypical behaviour in the consulting room. This will either be because she is not familiar with how she should behave in this situation or else she may be picking up your stress signals.
- If she is of an age to express her symptoms in a reasonably articulate fashion, let her do the talking. She should certainly answer the doctor's questions herself, although you may wish to add further salient facts.

Once the consultation is over and the diagnosis and follow-up treatment have been explained, you can continue to help her by:

- Discussing the visit in a positive way. Ask her what she thought about the visit, and reinforce the good bits and desensitize the less comfortable or unpleasant bits by explaining why they were needed.
- Being honest with her. If the medicine tastes unpleasant, there is no point in pretending that it is delicious. Follow it with something which she enjoys the taste of. If follow-up visits are required, you should say so, but only if she asks directly.

If there are related issues which worry you, or about which you need to know more, arrange to see the doctor without your child so you can discuss them fully. You will be able to tell her what she needs to know later. Don't overdo the attention or generate the expectation of a post-visit reward. There is no need for this, since you should avoid linking illness with reward.

Hospital

If your child is to be admitted as a planned in-patient, make sure you are familiar with all the arrangements concerning your own accommodation as well as the care plan for your child, so that you can explain in a simple, straightforward way what is going to happen. Give the young child as full an explanation as you can, but withhold any details which you feel will compromise how she might feel about going into hospital. It is worth getting hold of some books about hospital life to share ahead of the visit, but avoid a big build-up; a few days' notice is enough. A five-year-old needs to know:

- The treatment is designed to help her with something which is not quite right at the moment.
- You will be there all the time.
- Hospital is full of kind nurses and doctors who are there to help.
- She will come home just as soon as the doctor says she can.
- Lots of people spend time in hospital (name some she knows and say that they enjoyed their stay and are now better).

An eleven-year-old needs to know more about:

- The nature of the treatment.
- Its duration and likely effect.

Answers to direct questions should be truthful, but explained in a child-friendly way. Never promise a day for coming home to any child, whatever her age. This is beyond your control and she will hold you responsible for any disappointment.

Unplanned visits to hospital are traumatic for all concerned. If your child is well enough to ask questions, you can deal with each one factually and age-appropriately. Make no promises about how long she will be in the hospital or what treatment is likely, but do assure her that you will be on hand at all times. It can help to talk about your own unplanned hospital visits or those of other siblings/friends because it is reassuring to know that others have been in a similar situation. Explain what is happening on a step-by-step basis and remain overtly calm at all times.

Dentist

The British Dental Health Foundation (see Useful addresses, page 106) recommends that we all visit the dentist for a check-up at least once a year, ideally every six months.

With decay affecting more than half of children under five, it is particularly important that children are taken to the dentist early. Even babies without teeth should go along with their parents or older siblings in order to familiarize them with the sights, sounds and smells of modern dentistry, to help them to avoid developing dental anxiety later in life. Dental phobia is very common. You can help your child to avoid this by explaining:

- That the tools can make a noise because the dentist uses a special, very tiny drill to take away the bad bit of the tooth.
- That the drill is so quick it hardly takes a moment and it will not hurt. (Check privately with the dentist that this is the case before making this promise.)
- That the secret is to keep your mouth wide open because that helps the dentist to do his job quickly.
- That after the hole has been made and all the bad part of the tooth has gone the dentist will put in some filling to patch the

hole up. This will stop any toothache which might have followed if the hole had been left to get bigger.

Take the opportunity to reinforce the message that regular, effective teeth cleaning will help cut down the treatment needed, but it will not mean that you can stop going for regular check-ups.

Optician

Parents (and teachers) should look out for the following signs of an eyesight problem:

- skipping or re-reading lines or words
- reading unusually slowly
- holding material very close to the face
- turning or tilting the head so as to use only one eye
- using a pointer to mark the place long after reading has become second nature
- lacking the ability to remember what was read
- showing fatigue or listlessness when reading
- complaining about the print running together or jumping
- complaining of frequent headaches
- orienting drawings poorly on a page
- blinking frequently
- rubbing eyes excessively
- bumping into objects.

If your child needs glasses, considerable care should be taken in choosing the frames. Peers can be ruthless and the spectacles need to be viewed as a fashion-friendly accessory. Older children are technically able to wear contact lenses but these are high maintenance and not suitable for many youngsters.

Once glasses have been prescribed, she must wear them as instructed. Make sure school knows about them; they, and you, should take every opportunity to reinforce the benefits of wearing them. Listen to what she says about how others are responding to her having to wear them. If there is any sign of victimization step in straight away and talk to the teacher. It is essential that your child enjoys a lifetime of good vision and you will be compromising this if you allow her to become tardy in wearing her glasses for whatever reason.

Prescribed medicines and recreational drugs

It is better to offer drugs education in short, simple doses on a regular basis and within a meaningful context.

Your child needs to learn that some drugs (medicine) are good for her and some are not. You should tell her that when she is unwell you, or the doctor or nurse, give her medicine to help her get better. But add that if you take medicine when you are well it can make you feel unwell, and there are some drugs (be specific and refer to the good as medicine and the bad as drugs) which are never good for you. Tell her that to be safe she should only take medicine which has been given to her by an adult whom she knows very well.

There are lots of things we can do to keep our bodies healthy, like cleaning our teeth and eating fruit, but we must be careful not to hurt our bodies by taking medicine when we do not need it. If the issue of drugs crops up on the TV or elsewhere, and your child seems curious about this, you can take the opportunity to say: *That man is taking a drug which will harm his body. It will also make him behave in a way which might get him into trouble or danger and that is a bad thing to do.* If your child enquires further, answer her questions, but if the matter does not arise, let it drop until the next time it crops up in conversation. You need to be very clear about what your family views are about drug taking, and lead by example. If you have to take medicine in front of your child, explain what it is for and where you got it.

Older children need to be told that it is strong to say no if offered drugs or other stimulants, such as alcohol, before they are old enough. Peer pressure is very persuasive, and it is helpful to talk to your child about what it means to be a good friend so she understands that anyone offering drugs is certainly not a friend, because they are planning to harm their own body and they want someone else to do the same to theirs.

It can be very helpful if you encourage your child to participate in healthy activities such as sport, because prowess on the games field brings great kudos within the peer group.

Personal hygiene

It is important that children understand that disease and illness can be caused, or passed on, by very small organisms called germs, and that there are ways in which they can reduce their susceptibility to infection.

Some children become resistant to hand washing or bathing. It can help if you take time to explain that from the moment you finish washing your hands you begin to collect germs again since they are to be found on anything you touch. Do not, however, make such a big thing of germs that your child becomes obsessed with cleanliness. Just tell her that washing hands at particular times of the day will be effective in reducing the risk. Such times include after visiting the toilet, before eating and after touching a pet.

An effective hand-washing routine is to:

- Turn on the tap and wet your hands.
- Count to five while you scrub your hands with soap.
- Rinse under the running water while you count to five.
- Use a clean towel to dry your hands.

Taking regular baths helps to keep germs at bay but many children lose interest in bathing and it only resumes significance with the onset of puberty, at which point they can become preoccupied with how they are perceived by members of the opposite sex. During the cleanliness-resistant phase you need to be aware that shaming her into bathing will not be successful. Instead, you may consider reducing the bathing to two or three times a week on days which she chooses. Discuss which days you think are suitable contenders. Allow her to select personal bath products and set aside time when she can enjoy the bathroom facilities without interruption. Modesty should be respected, but safety not compromised.

Sun

Getting sunburnt as a child increases the risk of developing skin cancer later in life. The ears and neck are common problem sites and should be included in any sunscreen application. Children need to be told that the sun's ultraviolet rays cannot be seen but are dangerous, and that children can burn even on cloudy days and while in the shade.

It is important to establish good routines for times when exposure to sunlight is inevitable, and to discuss with your child why she should:

- Wear loose clothing, and a wide-brimmed hat which affords some protection to the back of the neck as well as to the face.
- Stay in the shade during the hottest part of the day – generally between 10.00 a.m. and 2.00 p.m.
- Have a sunscreen with a SPF of at least 15 applied about an hour before exposure and regularly during the day, especially if swimming.
- Drink plenty of water.
- Wear sunglasses with suitably approved lenses if she is troubled by the glare.

Water

When visiting, or playing, near water children should always be accompanied by an adult because it is a tragic fact that drowning is the second leading cause of unintentional injury-related death among children aged 14 and under. Children under 5 are at the highest risk. When taking a boat trip, all children, regardless of whether or not they can swim, should wear a buoyancy aid at all times and adults should lead by example. Children need to know that even strong swimmers can get into difficulties especially:

- If the water is very cold.
- If the distance she is trying to swim is too far for her strength, stamina and capability. It is worth adding that this is sometimes very difficult to judge from the shore or side of a pool.
- If the water becomes rough, the wind gets up or the tide or current is strong.
- If she swims on her own.
- If she walks out on thin ice.

Children should learn to swim as soon as it is feasible to take them to a pool. They can cope with lessons from about the age of 3. Water safety discussions should mention the following:

- Never run around the edge of the pool.
- Do not jump in on top of, or very near, someone else.
- Do not jump or dive into water unless you know for sure that it is deep enough.
- Do not swim unless there is an adult present.

Any infringement of these rules requires a serious discussion about the risks she is taking and which she is exposing others to. Make sure that any water-related garden feature is securely fenced off, and paddling pools should always be emptied after use.

Fire and fireworks

As soon as she can understand, you should tell her that matches are not something to play with and that if she finds any lying around she should give them to an adult. She also needs to know what she should do if she sees smoke or fire. We should tell children:

- To shout 'fire' in as loud a voice as possible and tell an adult what they have seen or smelt.
- To get out of the building as quickly as possible, and to crawl if there is a lot of smoke.
- Not to hide in a cupboard or under the bed.
- To go to a room with a window if they can't get out of the house. To put blankets or clothes against the bottom of the door to stop the smoke getting in and call for help out of the window.
- To find a phone and dial 999 if they can't tell a grown-up. They do not need money to make this call. To ask for the fire brigade and tell them where the smoke or fire is.
- Not to go back into the building to look for something.
- To drop to the floor and roll over and over if their clothes catch fire. If someone else's clothes are set alight they should use a rug, blanket or thick coat to help put out the flames.

All this makes very good sense, but you should make some routine, just-in-case, preparations:

- Make sure that children know at least two ways of getting out of the house quickly, and practise them from time to time.

- Tell them which room they should try to get to if there is a fire upstairs. It should have a phone in it.
- Make sure everyone knows where the keys to the doors and windows are kept.
- Tell them where you will meet if you have to get out of the house separately.
- Tell babysitters what to do in case of an emergency.

Fire prevention rules should include never:

- playing with candles
- playing close to a heater or lighted fire
- pulling on cables
- playing with sockets or electrical appliances
- putting anything on top of the cooker, heaters or lights.

Every year children start fires either accidentally or deliberately and some of them have fatal consequences. If your child is taking risks with fire the issue needs to be addressed. Do not ignore the situation or think that you can wait until she grows out of it. You should tell her:

- That fire is extremely dangerous and gets out of control faster than she can possibly imagine.
- That smoke, as well as fire, kills.
- That hoax 999 calls have meant that genuine cases have had to wait, with the result that people have suffered, and even died, needlessly.

The fire service may well be able to help via a member of staff with specialist training in how to help children who start fires. Children need to be given clear rules about how to behave where there are fireworks. The rules are straightforward and must never be broken:

- Adults light fireworks, not children.
- Fireworks scare pets, so keep them indoors.
- Fireworks should be kept in a secure tin, which has a lid.
- Stand well back from where the fireworks are being lit.
- No child under the age of 5 should be given a sparkler.
- If you are given a sparkler you must wear gloves, keep your arm

outstretched and place the sparkler in a bucket of water as soon as it is finished.

- Never go near a firework when it has been lit, even if it has not gone off. They can explode quite a long time after being lit.

The police

The police are there to help us and to enforce the law. They should not be used as a threat when your own discipline has proved ineffective, since this belittles their work and may cause your child to become unnecessarily frightened of them. Tell her about the kinds of things the police get involved with, but emphasize the positives. Saying that our roads are safer for everyone because the police make sure that people do not drive too fast, or in a way which is dangerous for them, or others, is a better lesson for life than cursing the speed cameras.

7

The wider world

Research indicates that if a child knows what is right he is more likely to try to do the right thing, but he will need much time, plenty of support and considerable experience before he can be relied upon to make responsible, independent decisions. Open-ended discussion will encourage him to consider alternative strategies and help him to develop deeper understanding.

Rights of self and others

Parents need to help their children to understand that, while their needs are important, so are those of other people.

There is a big difference between saying: *I need to feed the baby now, so you'll have to wait*, and: *I need to feed the baby now because he is hungry. You can be very helpful and play next to me while I do this. When I have finished feeding him we will read a story together.* Taking time to explain the full picture will help your child to see how he fits in and it will make him feel good about himself if, once the baby is fed, you were to go on to say: *That was very helpful of you. Thank you for playing quietly while I fed him. The baby is now comfortable and we can have some time together.*

As he matures, this approach can be applied more widely, with the focus moving gradually towards a recognition that we all have the right to contribute or participate: *I can see that you two cannot agree about the rules of the game. You have both got good ideas, but the game only works if you have rules which you both accept. How many rules do you think you need? Let's see if you can both decide on one each to start with, which the other one agrees is a good idea.* Any adult intervention should be even-handed because taking one person's view, without being seen to listen to everyone, is not the example you would wish your child to follow. Once the rules are agreed it would be worth saying: *You both handled that well. The game will be all the better because you agree on the rules and have made them up together.*

By the age of 7 or so children should begin to learn about the rights of individuals, starting from the perspective that we all share some basic needs, which are the same wherever you live, or whoever you are. Obvious ones are the need for food and shelter and for love and friendship. You might start a conversation by saying: *We agree that everyone needs somewhere to live. In a really fair world what would you think would be the most important things that every child should have?* Your child will probably list a bed, food, toys and other items which he uses on a daily basis. You can prompt him, if necessary, to think more abstractly: *How about the right to learn, to be safe and to choose his own friends?*

The next step is for you to establish that while we have rights, with them come responsibilities: *We have the right to have somewhere to live, and we also have a responsibility to look after it. We should all have the right to learn and we have the responsibility not to stop others from learning. We have the right to be safe and we must not do anything to hurt others. This means emotionally as well as physically.*

The world is not perfect and your child will inevitably face adversity. It will be beneficial if he learns from you about how to manage himself in such a situation. Recognizing that his rights are valid, but so are those of the other side, will help. An action plan should include:

- Accepting that there is a problem.
- Not resorting to physical means to express frustration.
- Allowing each party to say their piece without interruption.
- Listening neutrally.
- Exploring a range of solutions as suggested by both parties.
- Establishing a mutually acceptable course of action.
- Carrying out the action.

Diversity

Alongside learning about the rights people have, children need to be taught how to respect diversity. One of your objectives should be to help your child develop strategies which will equip him to deal with any prejudice which he might encounter, and to support those who experience it within his circle.

From an early age children notice the physical aspects of identity. This starts with gender and is followed by the identification of differences between their own physical appearance and those of other children. A conversation might be: *John has brown curly hair and yours is fair and straight. I like both kinds. You are both boys and both in Mrs Bloggs's class, so you are the same in some ways but different in others. Isn't it good that you are different? The world would be very boring if we were all the same. How would we know who was who?*

Potentially sensitive areas are:

- The composition of family groups. These can be single-parent, two-parent, same-sex adults or extended family.
- Racial and cultural issues. He may notice different physical attributes and become aware of different customs.

Reading stories with the young child which celebrate diversity will help to nurture a positive attitude. The older child will be very influenced by significant adults, their peers and the media. Parents must ensure that their input is consistently non-biased in favour of the status quo which exists within their own family.

Faith and belief

Intolerance stems from a lack of understanding. It is not possible for you to be fully acquainted with every religious faith or belief, but you should make it clear to your child that everyone has a right to believe what they wish and that we must respect this.

Point out places of worship and explain that special meetings are held there for people who belong to that particular community. Draw his attention to any media coverage of special celebrations conducted by different cultures and faiths.

Children may become aware that their friends respond to certain situations in a particular way because of their own beliefs, or those of their family. Explain that your child must respect this and not put pressure on his friend to change his lifestyle just because he wants him to behave in a different way. If this presents problems, suggest that your child asks his friend to talk more about his belief, what it means to him and what rituals he participates in so that a better understanding can develop between them.

Disability

Very young children will notice the more obvious physical disabilities and may ask questions about them. You should answer his questions as honestly as you can and in such a way that he does not become alarmed about disability. Always stress that just because one aspect of the disabled person's body does not work as ours does, this does not mean that he cannot think, talk, see, etc. as we do.

Young children will find those who are learning disabled or who live with disfigurement worrying. It is useful to explain that some people are born with this kind of problem, but that they receive a lot of help from their families and experts in the field and it is only right that they can go out and about like we do. Tell your child not to stare, but instead to smile at the disabled person if he or she looks his way.

It is useful to refer to the issue of everyone having rights within the context of a conversation about disability, since this may help an older child work out how he should respond when he comes face to face with a disabled person. Remind an older child that the disabled person will have feelings, hopes and fears just as we do, and that we must not be the one to hurt him or her or to make what is already a challenging life more difficult.

Always make time to answer your child's questions about disability because otherwise he may develop irrational views on the subject, which have the potential to develop into prejudice.

Poverty and privilege

Scenes involving extreme poverty feature regularly in the media. The coverage may focus on individual cases, or on whole countries, and is often designed to prompt us to donate money. While adults can rationalize their response to the tragic, and very moving sights shown on the television, a young child will not be able to. He may feel guilty about the apparent inequality in the world.

You will need to help him to understand that the pictures he is seeing are extreme and the fact that they are being shown on the television means that someone has already noticed that there is a problem and that help will be on the way. It is never a good idea to use such images to make your child feel guilty about leaving food or enjoying toys, a comfortable home and a good school, because this will make him feel frustrated about his inability to change things or cause him to lose interest rapidly. Instead, you might have a conversation about making a targeted donation to a particular cause: *I think the pictures we are seeing are very sad. Do you think it would be a good idea to work out how much we spend on our favourite meal and send this amount off to help the children we have seen in the news?*

If your older child seems particularly affected by what he has seen in the media you might suggest that he gives a small percentage of his birthday or pocket money to the cause.

The benefits which come with privilege may appear desirable on a superficial level, but children need to learn that it is quality, not quantity, which makes for a happy, balanced and fulfilling life.

Being discontented with one's lot, in a material sense, is not typical behaviour for the very young child. It may become an issue when the child has access to pocket money and is establishing his independence by spending social time with peers. In such groups inevitable comparisons about items of conspicuous consumption such as cars, clothes, holidays, etc. will be made and cult media programmes which promote affluent lifestyles will be discussed. The best way to deal with this is to stick to your budget and celebrate what you can afford by talking positively about your own assets. Tell your child that a wealthy lifestyle may appear to be wonderful on the surface, but some lottery winners have reported that their winnings have brought them little additional, long-term happiness. Avoid bemoaning any shortcomings in your own financial situation in front of your child. Enjoying a spontaneous treat with him will do wonders for everyone's morale.

The media

Advertising

Today's children are tomorrow's consumers but the advertising agencies know that adult spending is influenced by children long before they have money to spend. Before the age of about 6, children have difficulty in distinguishing between the artificial world of an advertisement and reality. They are easy targets since they are readily drawn into scenarios which promote a feel-good factor, or which imply that everyone must have a particular item in order to belong to the group.

If you feel that your child is being unduly influenced by an advertisement, you can talk to him about:

- How advertising actually works. Explain that the adverts represent a pretend world where no one ever quarrels with their friends or has to tidy their bedroom. Ask him if he thinks that buying a certain product will actually change his world significantly.
- The tricks advertisers use. Sometimes cartoon characters or celebrities are used to promote a product. Explain that celebrities will have been paid a lot of money just to say that they think that the product is marvellous and cartoon characters do not exist in the real world, so they will not need the featured item!
- How cross-marketing works – when a film is released, or a significant national occasion takes place, the market may well be awash with tie-in products. They benefit the product makers, and in all likelihood mementos will be consigned to the cupboard once the focus of attention becomes yesterday's news.
- How products are filmed to make them look much nicer than they actually are, particularly food.
- Even as the current advertisement is being given air time the marketing people are already planning their next promotion. We can't buy everything they recommend, so let's choose what we need for ourselves.

News

It should be remembered that news draws viewers because it covers the out of the ordinary, which is potentially disturbing for children since they are not always capable of setting stories within a context or appreciating the other side of a discussion.

There are a number of steps you can take to help your child avoid becoming overly sensitized by the news:

- Encourage him to watch children's news programmes.
- Discuss current affairs with him on a regular basis. Ask him his

opinion about events and why he thinks particular events have happened. In the interests of balance, include the positive and the banal, as well as the dramatic.

- Show how good can come out of bad because news stories have encouraged people to contribute positively after a natural disaster.
- Watch the news with him and filter unsuitable material.

Some items, for instance those covering extreme natural disasters or large-scale tragedies, can loom very large in a child's mind. Next time he experiences a thunderstorm, or a particularly windy day, he may worry that a hurricane or earthquake is about to hit. Items covering terrorist attacks, abductions, or school violence can cause him to worry about his own safety and that of his family and friends. You need to consider the following:

- The context of the disaster – do you know anyone who may have been directly affected, or who could be affected indirectly? For instance, if you have a family member who travels into the affected area every day, ascertain that they are safe so that you can reassure your child. If you are, or know of, a military family, make sure that your child knows that everyone is safe, or that there is a great deal of help in place to support those on site. If the disaster is associated with a mode of transport, you will need to explain that this is a very rare event compared to the total number of journeys, because otherwise your child may never want to use that form of travel again.
- If you are closely associated with someone who has been directly affected by the disaster, your child may take some time to show you how he is struggling to come to terms with the aftermath. In such a case you would be well advised to consult professional help for yourself as well as your child.
- The media will run a significant story almost continuously. It is best not to let your child see constant repeats. Nor should he watch events as they are unfolding or being repeated when he is alone. Many pictures of national disasters are too graphic for very young children.
- Always answer as factually as you can. While you should only supply information in answer to a direct question, and in an age-

appropriate way, you must avoid being over-protective, since his peers will probably want to discuss the situation. If your child has been suitably briefed, his friends will not make him feel anxious.

- Respect your child's feelings and fears but do not overreact and dwell only on the problems. Focus instead on how troubles and fears pass, by reminding him about something he used to worry about but which is no longer a problem. Tell him how good it is to face one's fears and to share them with someone.

Violence

Studies have shown that television can be a powerful influence in developing even a very young child's value systems and also in shaping his behaviour. In particular, research has proved that, over time, children may become immune to the horror of violence, or gradually come to believe that violence can be used to solve problems. They may also imitate the violence they see, and identify with either the perpetrator or the victim.

Parents can protect their children from these problems:

- By not having a television in your child's bedroom. Limit the time the child spends watching television; adhere to the watershed and check the content of the programmes he is watching.
- By watching DVDs and television with him.
- By pointing out that the programmes consist of actors pretending to fight in a studio with special effects, a film and sound crew on hand and body armour in place.
- By refusing to let him see a programme which is known to contain violent scenes and by turning it off if one comes on. Some explanation may be needed.
- By disapproving, in front of the children, of all violent episodes, stressing that such behaviour is not how you should go about settling problems.
- By contacting other parents to see if you can achieve a shared agreement that their children will also be prevented from watching unsuitable material. This will help to reduce the peer pressure which can motivate children to watch inappropriate programmes.

Conclusion: Good and bad choices

From an early age children need to make choices. Their ability to tell right from wrong develops as they mature and they will begin to appreciate the effect their choices have on other people. Parents can develop these decision-making skills by helping their child to make better informed decisions, and by discussing suitable ways of resisting peer pressure.

Choices facing young children are most likely to be those relating to play and friendships. Later these expand to include money, food, exercise, personal safety, health and the environment.

The young child must learn that she has to take turns and share toys. This lesson is not learnt over night and inevitably there will be many upsets along the way, but you should reward any positive behaviour choices with a congratulatory comment whenever you can. This positive feedback should include a mention of how much the other child will appreciate the kind thought which resulted in the good choice.

Playground disputes can be the cause of school-related anxiety and children may need to discuss these at home. Remember that, while it will be your natural inclination to side with your child, you will only be hearing her side of the story. It will be helpful if you ask her to recount everything from the other person's perspective as well as her own. Then you can discuss how she could have come up with a solution which may have required some compromise, but which would have meant that the playtime was happier for all.

Older children can learn from your reactions that careful consideration is essential when facing difficult decisions. You may feel tempted to give an immediate response to a request or statement of intent, but try to temper this, and instead engage your child in a discussion about her options. For instance, she needs to learn that pressure to behave in an unacceptable way can come from a variety of sources, including people she knows, and even someone she considers to be a friend. She also needs to learn that sometimes what is presented to her as fact is actually fiction.

It is also very beneficial for your child to learn how to be assertive. Assertiveness is born out of a feeling of confidence which, in turn, will be based on previous success in making effective choices. Over time children should learn that the right choice is more likely to come about by following this strategy:

- Pause
- Think
- Consider the options
- Weigh up the advantages and disadvantages of each option
- Predict the consequences
- Make a choice

If the wrong choice is made and the outcome presents difficulties, your child should feel safe in the knowledge that she can discuss it with you. Try to put the problem into perspective for her and establish at what stage the wrong choice was made. If necessary, help her to put things right. Once the analysis is complete, put it down to experience and move on.

Useful addresses

Action for Sick Children
36 Jacksons Edge Road
Disley
Stockport SK12 2JL
Freephone: 0800 0744519
Website: www.actionforsickchildren.org

Campaigns for better healthcare for children and teenagers, including issues such as hospital car-parking for parents. Produces booklets and leaflets for sick children, and those in hospital, and for their parents.

Blue Cross Pet Bereavement
Shilton Road
Burford
Oxfordshire
OX18 4PF
Helpline: 0800 096 6606
Website: www.bluecross.org.uk

British Association of Art Therapists
24–27 White Lion Street
London N1 9PD
Tel.: 020 7686 4216
Website: www.baat.org

Can give information about art therapy in your area.

British Dental Health Foundation
Smile House
2 East Union Street
Rugby
Warwickshire CV22 6AJ
Tel.: 0870 770 4000
Dental helpline: 0845 063 1188
Website: www.dentalhealth.org.uk

Seeks to raise public awareness of dental and oral health and to promote good dental-health practices.

British Society for Music Therapy
61 Church Hill Road
East Barnet
Hertfordshire EN4 8SY
Tel.: 020 8441 6226
Website: www.bsmt.org

Can put you in touch with a music therapist in your area.

Cancerbackup
3 Bath Place
Rivington Street
London EC2A 3JR
Helpline: 0808 800 1234
Website: www.cancerbackup.org.uk

Offers support and information about cancer, including useful booklets such as *What Do I Tell the Children?*

ChildLine
45 Folgate Street
London E1 6GL
Freephone helpline: 0800 1111 (24-hour)
Website: www.childline.org.uk

Offers help to children in trouble or danger, including bullying.

Children's Legal Centre
University of Essex
Wivenhoe Park
Colchester
Essex CO4 3SQ
Tel.: 01206 872466
Young People's Freephone: 0800 783 2187
Education Law Advice Line: 0845 456 6811
Website: www.childrenslegalcentre.com

Provides information and advice on parental responsibility and children's rights.

Cruse Bereavement Care
Cruse House
126 Sheen Road
Richmond
Surrey TW9 1UR
Helpline: 0870 167 1677
Freephone helpline for young people: 0808 808 1677
Website: www.crusebereavementcare.org.uk

Offers free, confidential help and support to bereaved people, including children, and publishes booklets on coping with grief which may be bought on-line.

Department for Education and Skills (DfES)
Sanctuary Buildings
Great Smith Street
London SW1P 3BT
Tel.: 0870 000 2288
Website: www.dfes.gov.uk/bullying

The department has produced an anti-bullying pack available to parents, teachers and young people.

Eating Disorders Association
First Floor, Wensum House
103 Prince of Wales Road
Norwich NR1 1DW
Tel.: 0845 634 7650 (for under-18s)
     0845 634 1414 (for over-18s)
Website: www.edauk.com

Education Otherwise
PO Box 325
Kings Lynn
Norfolk PE34 3XW
Helpline: 0870 730 0074 (staffed by volunteers)
Website: www.education-otherwise.org
Email: eoemailhelpline@education-otherwise.org

Provides information and support for parents who want to educate their children at home.

Family Welfare Association
501–505 Kingsland Road
London E8 4AU
Tel.: 020 7254 6251
Website: www.fwa.org.uk

Provides practical and emotional support for vulnerable and/or disadvantaged children and their parents.

Frank, the National Drugs Helpline
Helpline: 0800 77 66 00
Website: www.talktofrank.com

Free, confidential advice and information on drugs, available 24 hours a day.

Hyperactive Children's Support Group
Department W
71 Whyke Lane
Chichester
West Sussex PO19 7PD
Tel.: 01243 539966
Website: www.hacsg.org.uk

Kidscape
2 Grosvenor Gardens
London SW1W 0DH
Helpline: 08451 205 204
Website: www.kidscape.org.uk

Campaigns on all aspects of children's safety, and includes information about bullying and child abuse.

National Childminding Association of England and Wales
Royal Court
81 Tweedy Road
Bromley
Kent BR1 1TG
Tel.: 0845 880 0044
Website. www.ncma.org.uk

Gives information about helping your child settle in with a childminder.

NCH (the children's charity)
85 Highbury Park
London N5 1UD
Tel.: 0845 7626579 (9 a.m. to 5 p.m., Mondays to Fridays)
Website: www.nch.org.uk

National Family Mediation
7 The Close
Exeter EX1 1EZ
Tel.: 01392 271610
Website: www.nfm.u-net.com

Helps separating and divorcing couples to make the best arrangements for their children.

National Pyramid Trust for Children
84 Uxbridge Road
London W13 8RA
Tel.: 020 8579 5108
Website: www.nptrust.org.uk

Organizes 'Pyramid Clubs' through schools for children between the ages of 7 to 11 who seem withdrawn, isolated or to be having emotional problems; also provides parents' support groups.

National Self-Harm Network
PO Box 7264
Nottingham NG1 6WJ
Website: www.nshn.co.uk

National Society for the Prevention of Cruelty to Children (NSPCC)
Weston House
42 Curtain Road
London EC2A 3NH
Child Protection Helpline: 0808 800 5000 (24 hours)
Website: www.nspcc.org.uk

Parentline Plus
520 Highgate Studios
53–79 Highgate Road
London NW5 1TL
Helpline: 0808 800 2222
Website: www.parentlineplus.org.uk

Positive Parenting
2a South Street
Gosport
PO12 1ES
Tel.: 023 9252 8787
Website: www.parenting.org.uk

Provides leaflets for parents and professionals, and parenting workshops.

Relate
Herbert Gray College
Little Church Street
Rugby
Warwickshire CV21 3AP
Tel.: 01788 573241
Website: www.relate.org

Re-Solv
30a High Street
Stone
Staffordshire ST15 8AW
Helpline: 01785 817885
Website: www.re-solv.org (for parents)
　　　　　www.sniffing.org.uk (for young people)

Provides help for parents and children concerned about solvent abuse.

Royal Society for the Prevention of Accidents (RoSPA)
RoSPA House
Edgbaston Park
353 Bristol Road
Birmingham B5 7ST
Tel.: 0121 248 2000
Website: www.rospa.com

Provides information about accident prevention, and publishes a leaflet (Code HS 316) *Opportunities for Safety Education: A Guide to Principles and Practices for Childminders* (37p plus A5 s.a.e.)

Samaritans
The Upper Mill
Kingston Road
Ewell
Surrey KT17 2AF
Tel.: 08457 90 90 90
Website: www.samaritans.org.uk

Offers 24-hour totally confidential support and a listening ear to anyone in emotional distress.

Victim Support
Cranmer House
39 Brixton Road
London SW9 6DZ
Tel.: 0845 30 30 900
Website: www.victimsupport.org

Their trained volunteers can offer practical help and support to victims of crime.

Winston's Wish
The Clara Burgess Centre
Bayshill Road
Cheltenham
Gloucestershire GL50 3AW
Helpline: 08452 03 04 05
Website: www.winstonswish.org.uk

Supports bereaved children and young people.

Young Minds
48–50 St John Street
London EC1M 4DG
Tel.: 020 7336 8445
Parents Information Service: 0800 018 2138
Website: www.youngminds.org.uk

Supplies information on mental and emotional distress in young people.

Useful websites

www.childanxiety.net

www.parentscentre.gov.uk

www.raisingkids.co.uk

www.safekids.com

Index